Incredible Basketball Stories for Young Readers

15 Inspirational Tales From Basketball History for Kids

Trevor Fields

Table of Contents

Chapter 1:
Kobe Bryant: A Legacy of Excellence

Few names resonate as powerfully in professional sports as Kobe Bryant's. Known as the "Black Mamba," Kobe's career with the Los Angeles Lakers was nothing short of legendary, marked by incredible achievements, a relentless work ethic, and a deep love for the game. His journey from a young basketball prodigy to one of the greatest players in NBA history is a story of dedication, perseverance, and the relentless pursuit of greatness.

Kobe's passion for basketball was evident from a very young age. Born in Philadelphia, Pennsylvania, Kobe was introduced to the game by his father, Joe Bryant, a former professional basketball player. Growing up in Italy, where his father continued his professional career, Kobe was immersed in basketball, developing his skills and understanding of the game. Even as a child, Kobe's dedication to improving his game was unmatched; he would spend hours practicing, always striving to be the best.

When Kobe's family returned to the United States, his talent on the basketball court quickly became apparent. At Lower Merion High School in Pennsylvania, Kobe's performances were nothing short of spectacular, leading his team to a state championship and earning national recognition as one of the top high school players in the country. His incredible skills, combined with his competitive spirit, made him a standout player, attracting the attention of NBA scouts.

In 1996, Kobe made the bold decision to enter the NBA Draft straight out of high school, a move that was less common at the time but would pave the way for future generations of players. Drafted by the Charlotte Hornets and then traded to the Los Angeles Lakers, Kobe's NBA journey began with high expectations. From the outset, Kobe's talent was undeniable, but it was his work ethic and desire to be the best that set him apart. He was known for his intense practice sessions, his detailed study of the game, and his willingness to take the big shots in crucial moments.

Kobe's career with the Lakers was marked by incredible highs, including five NBA championships, two NBA Finals MVP awards, and 18 All-Star selections. His partnership with Shaquille O'Neal in the early 2000s led the Lakers to three consecutive championships, forming one of the most dominant duos in NBA history. Even after Shaq's departure, Kobe continued to lead the Lakers to success, cementing his legacy with two more championships in 2009 and 2010.

Beyond his achievements on the court, Kobe was known for his "Mamba Mentality" – a philosophy that focused on hard work, resilience, and the constant pursuit of excellence. Kobe's Mamba Mentality inspired not just basketball players but athletes and individuals across different fields, encouraging them to push beyond their limits and strive for greatness in all aspects of their lives.

Kobe Bryant's journey in the NBA was marked by a series of unforgettable performances that showcased his exceptional talent and unwavering determination. One of the most iconic moments in his career came on January 22, 2006, when Kobe scored an astonishing 81 points against the Toronto Raptors, the second-highest single-game scoring performance in NBA history. This remarkable feat exemplified Kobe's scoring ability and his refusal to back down, no matter the odds.

Kobe's excellence on the court was matched by his leadership and his ability to inspire his teammates. He was known for setting high standards, not just for himself but for everyone around him. Kobe's commitment to winning and his understanding of the game made him a natural leader, guiding the Lakers through challenging seasons and to ultimate victories. His ability to perform in clutch situations, hitting game-winning shots and making critical plays, earned him a reputation as one of the most reliable and fearless competitors in the league.

Off the court, Kobe was deeply involved in various charitable endeavors, using his platform to make a positive impact in the community. He was particularly passionate about youth sports and education, founding the Kobe and Vanessa Bryant Family Foundation to help young people achieve their full potential. Kobe's philanthropic efforts extended globally, including significant contributions to after-school programs, scholarship funds, and sports-related initiatives.

Kobe's influence also reached beyond basketball, touching the worlds of literature, film, and business. His love for storytelling led him to win an Academy Award for his animated short film "Dear Basketball," which beautifully captured his love for the game and his farewell to the sport that defined much of his life. Kobe's ventures into business and media further showcased his creativity and entrepreneurial spirit, demonstrating that his ambitions and talents were not confined to the basketball court.

Kobe Bryant's career was also defined by his resilience and ability to overcome adversity. Throughout his time in the NBA, he faced numerous challenges, including injuries and team dynamics, that tested his resolve and commitment to the game. Yet, Kobe's response to these obstacles only added to his legend, showcasing his mental toughness and dedication to excellence.

One of the most significant tests of Kobe's career was the transition period following the departure of Shaquille O'Neal from the Lakers in 2004. With the team in a rebuilding phase, Kobe emerged as the undisputed leader, taking on the challenge of guiding a young team through the highs and lows of the NBA season. His leadership during this time was a testament to his growth as a player and a person, embodying the "Mamba Mentality" of facing challenges head-on and striving to bring out the best in those around him.

Kobe's commitment to improving his game and his relentless work ethic were evident in his approach to training and preparation. Known for his early morning workouts and exhaustive study of the game, Kobe set a standard for what it meant to be a professional athlete. His dedication to mastering every aspect of basketball, from footwork and shooting to defense and conditioning, inspired a generation of players to adopt a similar approach to their craft.

Beyond his individual achievements and accolades, Kobe's greatest legacy may be the inspiration he provided to countless fans and aspiring athletes. His "Mamba Mentality" - a philosophy centered around the pursuit of excellence, resilience in the face of adversity, and the relentless pursuit of one's goals - became a guiding principle for many, both within and outside the world of sports. Kobe's message was clear: greatness is not handed to you; it is earned through hard work, dedication, and an unwavering belief in oneself.

Kobe's impact on the game of basketball and his contributions to society continued even after his retirement in 2016. Through his coaching, storytelling, and philanthropic efforts, Kobe remained committed to inspiring and empowering the next generation. His untimely passing in January 2020 left a void in the world of sports and beyond, but his legacy lives on, a testament to the incredible impact one individual can have.

Kobe Bryant's influence extended well beyond the final buzzer of his last game. Known for his "Mamba Mentality," this mindset wasn't just about pushing the limits on the basketball court; it was a comprehensive approach to life that emphasized passion, dedication, and continuous improvement. This philosophy inspired not only athletes across various sports but also individuals striving for excellence in their personal and professional lives.

One of the most touching aspects of Kobe's legacy is his role as a mentor and advocate for women's basketball. His support for the WNBA and young female athletes was evident through his attendance at games and public encouragement of rising stars. Kobe's dedication to advancing women's sports was also deeply personal, reflected in his close relationship with his daughter Gianna, who shared his love for basketball and aspired to follow in his footsteps. Their shared dream underscored Kobe's belief in the potential of every athlete, regardless of gender, to achieve greatness.

Kobe's creative pursuits off the court showcased his multifaceted talents and interests. His foray into the world of storytelling, including his Academy Award-winning short film "Dear Basketball," revealed a deeply reflective and artistic side to Kobe that many fans hadn't seen before. This project, among others, demonstrated Kobe's commitment to exploring new challenges and expressing his love for the game in innovative ways.

Kobe's business ventures further exemplified his visionary approach to life after basketball. From investment in sports drinks to youth sports training facilities, his endeavors were not just about financial success but about making a meaningful impact on future generations. Kobe's involvement in the tech world and his support for startups showed his belief in the power of innovation and his desire to contribute to the growth and development of new ideas.

As we close the chapter on Kobe Bryant, we reflect on a legacy that transcends statistics, records, and championships. Kobe's journey from a basketball prodigy to an NBA legend and cultural icon is a narrative filled with lessons of resilience, passion, and the relentless pursuit of excellence. His "Mamba

Mentality" has become a beacon for aspiring athletes and individuals across various fields, embodying the essence of dedication and the continuous quest for greatness.

Kobe's impact on basketball is undeniable. His five NBA championships, numerous All-Star appearances, and countless breathtaking performances on the court have cemented his place among the game's all-time greats. Yet, it's his contributions off the court that have profoundly shaped his enduring legacy. From his advocacy for women's sports and his ventures into storytelling and business to his philanthropic efforts, Kobe demonstrated a commitment to making a positive impact in the world.

The tragic loss of Kobe, his daughter Gianna, and the other passengers in a helicopter accident in January 2020 left the world in mourning. The outpouring of love and respect in the aftermath of the tragedy highlighted the deep connection Kobe had forged with fans around the globe and the widespread impact of his life and career. Tributes poured in from all corners, not just from the basketball community but from individuals and organizations touched by his spirit and generosity.

Kobe's legacy is a complex tapestry woven from his triumphs and challenges, his public persona and private endeavors. It's a legacy that encourages us to face our fears, to rise after we fall, and to embrace the journey toward our goals with unwavering determination. Kobe taught us that greatness is not a destination but a journey, marked by continuous effort, learning, and growth.

Kobe's story is a powerful testament to the impact one individual can have, not just in their chosen field but as a force for positive change in the world. His "Mamba Mentality" lives on, inspiring us to strive for excellence, to be passionate about our pursuits, and to leave an indelible mark on the world, just as Kobe did.

Chapter 2:
Wilt Chamberlain Scores 100 Points

∞

Wilt Chamberlain's basketball career was filled with more accolades than that of nearly anyone who has ever played the sport. Yet, among his numerous achievements, one night stands out—a night when Wilt transcended the sport itself to etch his name into eternity. This is the story of how he scored an astounding 100 points in a single game.

Wilt, affectionately known as "The Big Dipper" for his towering presence and the way he seemed to scoop up points with ease, was a force of nature on the basketball court. His combination of height, strength, and agility was unparalleled, making him a formidable opponent for any team. But on the night of March 2, 1962, in a modest arena in Hershey, Pennsylvania, Wilt was to undertake a journey from being merely a basketball player to becoming a legend.

The game was set between Wilt's team, the Philadelphia Warriors, and their rivals, the New York Knicks. The stage was far from glamorous—the gym was modest, the crowd was small, and the media attention minimal. Little did anyone know, they were about to witness history.

From the opening tip-off, Wilt dominated the game with an air of inevitability. Each leap towards the basket, each graceful arc of the ball, seemed to whisper hints of the extraordinary. Wilt's movements were a dance, his scoring spree a melody that resonated through the gym, captivating the audience with its rhythm and intensity.

As the game progressed, Wilt's teammates, caught up in the unfolding spectacle, began to feed him the ball at every opportunity. They recognized the magic of the moment, each pass a brushstroke in a masterpiece that was coming to life before their eyes. The synergy between Wilt and his teammates was palpable, a testament to their collective desire to be part of something greater than themselves.

With every basket Wilt scored, the energy in the gym swelled. The crowd, initially just spectators, became participants in this historic endeavor, their cheers a chorus that spurred Wilt on. The scoreboard ticked upwards, and with it, the anticipation grew. The realm of the possible expanded with each point Wilt scored, as the unthinkable slowly started to seem inevitable.

Wilt's scoring was not just a display of physical prowess; it was an exhibition of mental fortitude. The pressure of the moment, the weight of potential history on his shoulders, would have buckled many. But Wilt, with a focus as unwavering as his skill, pressed on. His determination was as much a part of this story as his talent, a reminder that the path to greatness is paved with resilience as well as skill.

As the game neared its end, and Wilt's point tally soared into the nineties, the atmosphere in the gym was electric. Each possession was charged with the tension and excitement of the imminent. The Knicks, despite their best efforts, were powerless to stem the tide of Wilt's scoring. They, too, were caught up in the spectacle, unwitting participants in a drama that transcended the rivalry of the game.

Wilt's approach to the century mark was a crescendo, each point building on the last, driving the narrative forward with unstoppable momentum. The crowd, on the edge of their seats, could hardly believe what they were witnessing. The air was thick with anticipation, each breath shared by players and spectators alike, united in the suspense of the moment.

In those final minutes, as Wilt inched closer to the 100-point mark, the sense of collective anticipation was palpable. Each shot, each successful basket, brought him closer to a milestone that seemed as much a feat of will as it was of skill. The tension was a tangible force, a shared experience that bound everyone in the gym in a singular, breathless wait.

As the game hurtled toward its historic conclusion, the atmosphere in the small gym in Hershey, Pennsylvania, was electric with anticipation. The crowd, a mix of curious locals and die-hard basketball fans, realized they were on the cusp of witnessing something unprecedented. Wilt Chamberlain, already a towering figure in the game, was about to transcend into a legend.

Wilt's performance that night was a symphony of basketball prowess. Each move he made, each shot he took, was a note in an unfolding epic of athletic excellence. The crowd, fully attuned to the gravity of the moment, watched in rapt attention as Wilt moved closer to a milestone that seemed almost otherworldly.

The energy in the gym was palpable, a tangible buzz that seemed to fuel Wilt's determination. With every basket, the excitement grew, a collective sense of witnessing history in the making. The anticipation was not just about the achievement of scoring 100 points but also about seeing the limits of what was thought possible being pushed further.

Wilt's teammates, fully aware of the historic pace at which the game was unfolding, rallied around him. Each pass to Wilt was more than just an assist; it was an acknowledgment of their collective pursuit of greatness. The camaraderie and unspoken bond between them were evident, a testament to the power of teamwork and shared goals.

As the points piled up, the game transformed. It was no longer just a contest between two teams; it had become a stage for an extraordinary individual performance. Yet, despite the focus on Wilt's scoring feat, the essence of the game remained intact. The fluid back-and-forth, the defense and offense, the sound of the ball against the hardwood—all these elements combined to create a spectacle that was about more than just the numbers.

The opposing team, the New York Knicks, found themselves in a unique position. While they were the adversaries for the night, they were also part of a historic moment. Their efforts to stem Wilt's scoring tide added to the drama, providing the resistance that made each of Wilt's points all the more remarkable.

As the final quarter began, the sense of inevitability grew stronger. Wilt was not just chasing a personal best; he was on the verge of redefining what was possible in basketball. Each successful shot brought a roar from the crowd, a mixture of disbelief and admiration for the man who was rewriting the record books in real-time.

The tension and excitement built with each passing minute, reaching a crescendo as Wilt neared the 100-point mark. The anticipation was almost unbearable, each moment stretching out as the crowd waited for the inevitable. And then, with a grace that belied the pressure of the moment, Wilt scored his 100th point.

The reaction was immediate and overwhelming. The crowd erupted in a frenzy of cheers and applause, a spontaneous outpouring of joy for a feat that many had thought impossible. The players on the court, both teammates and opponents, paused to acknowledge the magnitude of the moment, joining in the celebration of an achievement that transcended team rivalries.

In the midst of the celebration, Wilt's teammates lifted him high, a hero not just of the game but of the sport itself. The image of Wilt, triumphant and smiling, holding a handwritten sign that read "100," would become an iconic symbol of individual achievement and the limitless potential of human endeavor.

As the gym slowly returned to calm, the realization set in. Wilt Chamberlain's 100-point game was more than just a record; it was a landmark moment in sports history, a testament to the power of ambition, perseverance, and the relentless pursuit of excellence. It was a reminder that in the realm of sports, as in life, the impossible is only a challenge waiting to be overcome.

In the aftermath of Wilt Chamberlain's monumental achievement, the world of basketball found itself at a crossroads of history and possibility. The echoes of Wilt's 100-point game reverberated far beyond the walls of the Hershey Sports Arena, igniting conversations and debates in every corner where basketball was played or cherished. This wasn't just about a new benchmark in scoring; it was a moment that expanded the horizons of what athletes could aspire to achieve.

As the news of Wilt's feat spread, it captured the imagination of players and fans alike, from the bustling courts of urban America to the makeshift hoops in remote corners of the world. Young players, shooting hoops in their backyards or local parks, now had a new figure of inspiration. Wilt's story was not just one of talent and achievement but also of breaking barriers and redefining the limits of success in sports.

The impact of Wilt's 100-point game was felt not just in the immediate aftermath but in the years and decades that followed. It became a pivotal point of reference for players who followed in Wilt's footsteps, a beacon that guided them in their pursuit of excellence. Legends of the game, from Michael Jordan to LeBron James, have spoken of Wilt's influence on their careers, citing his achievements as a source of motivation and a benchmark for their success.

Beyond its significance as a record, Wilt's 100-point game challenged the very philosophy of basketball. Coaches and strategists were prompted to rethink their approaches to the game, considering new tactics and strategies that could accommodate such extraordinary individual performances. The game also highlighted the importance of teamwork and collaboration, as Wilt's teammates played a crucial role in facilitating his historic scoring spree.

In the broader cultural context, Wilt's achievement transcended the realm of sports to become a symbol of excellence and perseverance. It served as a reminder that with hard work and dedication, seemingly insurmountable goals could be achieved. This message resonated with people from all walks of life, making Wilt's 100-point game a source of inspiration for individuals facing their challenges and striving for their personal best.

As the years passed, the legacy of Wilt's 100-point game continued to grow, becoming a cherished part of basketball folklore. The game's significance was commemorated in various ways, from documentaries and books to special events and tributes. The story of that night in Hershey became a rite of passage for young basketball fans, a tale passed down from one generation to the next, imbued with the magic and wonder of the sport.

Wilt's 100-point game stands as a monument to human potential and the enduring spirit of competition. It is a testament to the idea that sports are not just about winning or losing but about pushing the boundaries of what is possible and inspiring others to do the same.

As we reflect on Wilt Chamberlain's unparalleled achievement, we are reminded of the power of sports to unite, inspire, and elevate. Wilt's 100-point game is not just an impressive record; it is a beacon of hope and a source of inspiration, a story that continues to captivate and motivate those who dare to dream of achieving the impossible.

Chapter 3:
The Rise of Michael Jordan

∞

In the world of basketball, few names shine as brightly as Michael Jordan's. His journey from a young boy with big dreams to becoming one of the greatest basketball players of all time is a story of determination, hard work, and incredible talent. But Michael's journey wasn't always easy, and it's filled with lessons about never giving up, no matter how tough things get.

Michael Jordan's story begins in Wilmington, North Carolina, where he was just another kid who loved playing sports. Basketball, baseball, and football were all part of his life, but there was something about basketball that captured his heart. Michael had a natural talent for the game, but what set him apart even more was his relentless work ethic. He practiced for hours, shooting hoops in his backyard, determined to get better every day.

One of the most pivotal moments in Michael's early life came when he was in high school. In a twist that seems almost unbelievable given his future success, Michael was cut from his high school varsity basketball team. Instead of letting this setback defeat him, Michael used it as fuel to work even harder. He made the junior varsity team and became a standout player, proving to everyone, especially himself, that he had what it takes to succeed.

Michael's high school years were just the beginning. His hard work and dedication paid off when he was offered a basketball scholarship to the University of North Carolina (UNC), a school known for its strong basketball program. At UNC, Michael's talent truly began to shine. In his very first season, he helped lead his team to the national championship, hitting the game-winning shot in the final seconds of the championship game. This moment was a glimpse of the clutch performances Michael would become famous for throughout his career.

But Michael's rise to basketball greatness was about more than just his on-court skills. He was known for his competitive spirit and his refusal to settle for anything less than the best from himself and his teammates. His time at UNC was marked by hard work, both in practice and in games, and his drive to improve was relentless. Michael wasn't just playing to win; he was playing to become the best.

As Michael's college career progressed, he racked up awards and recognition, becoming one of the most talked-about college players in the country. His incredible performances and game-winning plays made it clear that he was ready for the next level. After three years at UNC, Michael made the decision to enter the NBA Draft, a move that would start the next chapter in his legendary basketball journey.

The NBA was a whole new challenge, but Michael was ready. Drafted by the Chicago Bulls, he quickly made a name for himself in the league with his breathtaking dunks, incredible scoring ability, and unmatched competitive fire. From his very first season, it was clear that Michael wasn't just another rookie; he was a force to be reckoned with, a player who could change the course of a game in an instant.

Michael's early years in the NBA were filled with personal success, but team success was harder to come by. The Bulls struggled to make it deep into the playoffs, often facing tough competition that seemed just out of reach. But Michael never gave up. He continued to push himself and his teammates, believing that with enough hard work and determination, they could become champions.

As Michael Jordan's journey in the NBA unfolded, his extraordinary abilities on the basketball court became the stuff of legend. Each game was a new opportunity for Michael to showcase his talent, and he seized these opportunities with both hands. His acrobatic dunks, lightning-fast steals, and incredible scoring runs captivated fans and struck fear into the hearts of opponents.

Yet, the road to true greatness in the NBA is seldom smooth, and Michael faced his share of hurdles. The Chicago Bulls, despite having a gem like Jordan, weren't initially a championship-caliber team. They faced formidable opponents, particularly in the Eastern Conference, where fierce rivals awaited at every turn. Games were hard-fought battles, and victories were earned, not given.

In these early NBA days, Michael's resolve was tested. Despite his individual success, including numerous All-Star appearances and scoring titles, the ultimate prize—a championship—remained elusive. Basketball, after all, is a team sport, and it was clear that for the Bulls to reach the pinnacle of success, they needed to grow not just as individual players but as a unified team.

The transformation of the Chicago Bulls into a championship team is a testament to Michael's leadership and the collective spirit of the team. Michael's work ethic was infectious; his dedication to practice, his commitment to excellence, and his refusal to accept defeat inspired his teammates to elevate their own games. The Bulls began to coalesce into a more formidable unit, each player contributing to a greater whole.

One of the turning points in Michael's career, and indeed in the history of the Chicago Bulls, came with the arrival of Phil Jackson as head coach. Jackson introduced a new offensive strategy, the triangle offense, which emphasized passing, movement, and versatility. This system was a perfect fit for Michael's skills, allowing him greater freedom to create plays and utilize his strengths to the team's advantage.

Under Jackson's guidance, the Bulls' transformation continued. Scottie Pippen, one of Michael's most trusted teammates, emerged as a star in his own right, providing the Bulls with a potent one-two punch. Together, Michael and Scottie became one of the most dynamic duos in basketball history, their complementary styles of play propelling the Bulls to new heights.

The culmination of Michael's early years in the NBA came when the Bulls finally broke through the barrier that had held them back. In 1991, after years of hard-fought battles and playoff disappointments, the Chicago Bulls won their first NBA Championship. Michael's joy was uncontainable, a raw, emotional release after years of striving for this moment. This victory was more than just a win; it was the realization of Michael's dream and the reward for his unwavering dedication.

The Bulls' championship victory was a turning point, not just for the team, but for Michael's legacy. It silenced critics who had questioned his ability to lead a team to the ultimate success. More importantly, it solidified Michael's belief in the power of perseverance, teamwork, and never giving up, no matter the odds.

The Chicago Bulls' first championship in 1991 was just the beginning of what would become one of the most remarkable dynasties in NBA history. With Michael Jordan leading the charge, the Bulls were not content with a single title. They hungered for more, driven by a collective desire to prove their dominance in the basketball world.

The following years saw the Bulls solidify their status as an NBA powerhouse. Michael, along with Scottie Pippen and a roster of talented and dedicated players, worked tirelessly to maintain their edge. Each season, they approached the game with the same intensity and determination that had brought them their first championship. The Bulls' playing style, a blend of skill, teamwork, and an unbreakable will to win, made them a formidable force on the court.

Michael's leadership was instrumental in the Bulls' continued success. He was not just their star player; he was the heart and soul of the team. Michael set the standard for excellence, pushing himself and his teammates to always strive for greatness. His competitive spirit was infectious, and it drove the Bulls to achieve heights that few teams in NBA history have reached.

The early 1990s saw the Bulls capture three consecutive NBA championships, a feat that cemented their dynasty and Michael's place in basketball lore. These championship runs were marked by memorable moments and clutch performances that highlighted Michael's incredible talent and his ability to rise to the occasion when it mattered most.

One of the most iconic moments of Michael's career came during the 1992 NBA Finals against the Portland Trail Blazers. In the first half of Game 1, Michael put on a shooting clinic, hitting six three-pointers and shrugging in disbelief at his own hot hand. This image of Michael, shrugging as if to say he couldn't even explain his own brilliance, became an enduring symbol of his greatness.

But Michael's impact on the game went beyond his scoring ability. He was a tenacious defender, a gifted passer, and a leader who could inspire his team to rally from behind. His all-around game was a testament to his dedication to being the best player he could be, in every facet of the game.

Michael was not just a basketball player, but a global icon. He was a symbol of excellence and determination. His endorsement deals, most notably with Nike, helped to make him one of the most recognizable athletes in the world. He was a cultural phenomenon, whose impact transcended the sport.

The Bulls' dynasty of the 1990s, with their six championships, is a testament to what can be achieved when talent meets hard work and determination. Michael Jordan's rise from a young boy with a dream to the pinnacle of basketball greatness is a story that inspires not just athletes but anyone who strives to achieve their best in the face of challenges.

The legacy of Michael Jordan extends far beyond the confines of basketball courts and the records he shattered. His influence on the game of basketball, sports culture, and the very notion of what it means to strive for excellence continues to resonate long after his retirement.

Michael Jordan redefined what it meant to be a professional athlete. His work ethic, competitive spirit, and dedication to improvement set a new standard for what athletes across all sports aspired to. His mantra of never giving up, even in the face of failure, became a beacon for countless individuals, both within and outside the sports world.

The impact of Michael's career on future generations of basketball players is immeasurable. He inspired a whole new generation to pick up a basketball, to dream big, and to work hard towards those dreams. Players like Kobe Bryant, LeBron James, and many others have spoken about how Michael's legacy motivated them to reach the heights of basketball greatness. They emulated his dedication to the game, his relentless pursuit of victory, and his ability to perform under pressure.

Beyond individual players, Michael's influence reshaped the NBA and basketball around the world. His global appeal helped popularize the NBA internationally, bringing the game to new audiences and inspiring a global community of fans and players. Basketball leagues and programs sprouted up worldwide, each echoing the excitement and passion that Michael brought to the game.

Off the court, Michael Jordan became a cultural icon, his influence permeating areas like fashion, business, and philanthropy. His Air Jordan brand transformed the sneaker industry, blending sports, fashion, and personal branding in a way that was unprecedented. Michael's ventures into business and ownership have also set examples for athletes looking to build their legacies beyond their playing days.

Moreover, Michael's charitable efforts, including contributions to education, community building, and healthcare, demonstrate his commitment to giving back and making a difference in the lives of others. His legacy is not just in the records he set or the championships he won but also in the lives he touched and the communities he helped build.

Michael's legacy is one that transcends basketball, embodying the essence of what it means to strive for and achieve greatness. The spirit of Michael Jordan's journey continues to inspire, reminding us all of the heights we can reach when we dare to dream and work tirelessly towards turning those dreams into reality.

Chapter 4:
Kareem Abdul-Jabbar:
Basketball's Scoring Machine

∞

Few names in basketball history shine as brightly as Kareem Abdul-Jabbar. His story is not just one of scoring points; it's a tale of resilience, intellect, and the pursuit of excellence both on and off the court. Kareem's journey to setting scoring records is a testament to his skill, dedication, and the iconic skyhook shot that became his signature move.

Born Ferdinand Lewis Alcindor Jr. in New York City, Kareem was a standout player from his early days. Even as a young boy, his talent on the basketball court was undeniable. Towering over his peers, he moved with a grace and skill that belied his size. Kareem's high school career was marked by unprecedented success, leading his team to three straight New York City Catholic Championships and capturing the attention of college scouts nationwide.

Kareem's college years at UCLA under the legendary coach John Wooden were a harbinger of the greatness to come. His time with the Bruins was nothing short of spectacular, leading the team to three consecutive national championships. But Kareem's impact went beyond just winning games. He was a student of the game, absorbing lessons from Coach Wooden not just on basketball strategy but on life itself. His college years were a time of growth, both as an athlete and as a person, shaping the principles he would carry throughout his career.

Entering the NBA in 1969, Kareem's arrival was met with great anticipation. Drafted by the Milwaukee Bucks, he made an immediate impact, earning Rookie of the Year honors and quickly establishing himself as one of the league's premier talents. Kareem's presence on the court was commanding, his basketball IQ off the charts, and his scoring ability unmatched. But it was his signature move, the skyhook, that would become the stuff of legend.

The skyhook, a graceful, arching shot, was virtually unstoppable. Kareem would release the ball at the highest point of his reach, making it nearly impossible for defenders to block. This move, combined with his agility and basketball smarts, made Kareem a scoring powerhouse, consistently leading him to be among the top scorers season after season.

But Kareem's journey wasn't without its challenges. The NBA was evolving, and the competition was fierce. Teams like the Boston Celtics and the Los Angeles Lakers were powerhouses, filled with talent that tested Kareem's resolve and the Bucks' ability to contend for championships. Yet, through every trial, Kareem remained focused, dedicated to honing his craft and elevating his game.

Kareem's move to the Los Angeles Lakers in 1975 marked a new chapter in his career. In the City of Angels, Kareem found a new home and a new team to lead. The Lakers, with Kareem at the helm, became a dominant force in the NBA, captivating fans with their skill, teamwork, and the sheer brilliance of Kareem's play. His partnership with Magic Johnson, another basketball legend, was magical, their on-court synergy propelling the Lakers to multiple championships.

Through the years, Kareem's consistency and excellence never wavered. Season after season, he was a model of reliability and skill, his scoring records piling up until he reached the pinnacle: basketball's all-time leading scorer (only to be passed by LeBron James in 2023). This achievement wasn't just a testament to Kareem's scoring ability; it was a reflection of his longevity, his ability to adapt and excel in an ever-changing game.

Kareem's impact on basketball extends beyond just points and championships. He was a pioneer, a player who brought intellect and contemplation to the game, challenging perceptions and advocating for change both within and outside the sport. His contributions to basketball are immeasurable, not just in the records he set but in the example he provided for future generations.

Kareem Abdul-Jabbar's contributions to basketball are not limited to his remarkable scoring ability or his championships. His journey in the NBA is also a story of evolution, adaptability, and the pursuit of knowledge, both on and off the court. Kareem's intellectual approach to the game, combined with his physical prowess, made him a unique figure in the world of sports.

During his time with the Los Angeles Lakers, Kareem continued to refine his game, adding new dimensions to his play. His defensive skills became as formidable as his offensive talents, earning him multiple selections to the NBA All-Defensive Teams. Kareem's ability to alter opponents' shots and dominate the boards was a key factor in the Lakers' defensive strategy, complementing his scoring contributions.

Kareem's work ethic was legendary. He was known for his rigorous fitness regimen and his commitment to staying in peak physical condition. This dedication to his health and his craft was one of the reasons for his remarkable longevity in the league. Kareem played 20 seasons in the NBA, a testament to his ability to maintain a high level of play well into the latter stages of his career.

Beyond his physical preparation, Kareem was a student of the game. He studied film, analyzed opponents, and was always looking for ways to improve. His keen understanding of basketball strategy made him a valuable leader on the court, guiding his teammates and making smart plays that contributed to the team's success.

Kareem's leadership extended beyond the court. He was a mentor to younger players, sharing his knowledge and experience to help them develop their skills. His partnership with Magic Johnson is a prime example of this mentorship. Kareem's guidance helped shape Magic's game, and their collaboration brought out the best in both players, leading to multiple championships for the Lakers.

Off the court, Kareem was just as impactful. He was an outspoken advocate for social justice, using his platform to raise awareness about issues affecting the African American community and society at large. Kareem's activism was rooted in his deep sense of justice and his desire to make a positive impact beyond basketball.

Kareem's interests extended into the world of arts and culture. He was an avid reader, a jazz enthusiast, and a writer. His intellectual pursuits enriched his life and provided a balance to the demands of his basketball career. Kareem's love for learning and his engagement with a wide range of interests made him a well-rounded individual, admired not just for his athletic achievements but also for his contributions to culture and society.

As Kareem's career progressed, his legacy as one of the game's all-time greats became increasingly clear. His scoring records, MVP awards, and championships were tangible measures of his success, but his influence on the game and on those who played it was immeasurable. Kareem Abdul-Jabbar was not just a basketball player; he was an ambassador for the sport, a role model for athletes, and a voice for positive change in the community.

As Kareem's career approached its twilight, his legacy as one of basketball's greatest players was already secure. However, Kareem wasn't one to rest on his laurels; he continued to play with the same passion and dedication that had marked his entire career. It was this unwavering commitment to excellence that allowed him to achieve his scoring records.

These monumental achievements didn't come easily. It was the result of years of hard work, constant improvement, and an undying love for the game. Kareem's records were a testament to his skill, longevity, and consistent performance at the highest level of basketball. Each point he scored was a step towards etching his name in the annals of basketball history, and when he finally surpassed the previous scoring record, it was a moment of triumph not just for Kareem but for the sport as a whole.

But Kareem's influence on basketball extends far beyond just his scoring ability. He was a pioneer in many ways, reshaping the center position with his unmatched skill set. His finesse, basketball IQ, and the unstoppable skyhook shot set new standards for future generations of players. Kareem showed that being a center wasn't just about size and strength; it was about skill, agility, and intelligence.

Throughout his career, Kareem faced off against some of the toughest competitors the NBA had to offer. From fierce rivalries with other teams to friendly duels with fellow players, Kareem's journey was marked by memorable matchups that showcased the competitive spirit of basketball. These encounters, against the backdrop of the NBA's evolving landscape, highlighted Kareem's adaptability and his ability to excel in a changing game.

Kareem's retirement from professional basketball was a significant moment for the sport. It marked the end of an era, but also the beginning of his lasting legacy. Kareem left behind a record that would stand as a benchmark for excellence, a goal for future players to aspire to. His departure from the court didn't diminish his influence on the game; if anything, it allowed his contributions to be viewed in a broader, more impactful light.

Off the court, Kareem's legacy continued to grow. He became an advocate for education, social justice, and cultural understanding. Kareem's voice, once known for calling plays and leading teams, became a beacon for change, addressing issues that extended far beyond the basketball court. His commitment to making a positive impact in the community showed that Kareem's greatness wasn't confined to his athletic achievements; it was also reflected in his character and his actions.

The enduring legacy of Kareem Abdul-Jabbar extends far beyond the hardwood floors of basketball courts and the record books of the NBA. His journey from a young, talented player to a seasoned veteran and all-time leading scorer is a narrative rich with lessons in perseverance, intellectual curiosity, and social advocacy. Kareem's impact on basketball is undeniable, but his influence on society and culture is equally profound.

Kareem's retirement from professional basketball was not an end but a transition to new avenues through which he could inspire and educate. His post-basketball career has been marked by a commitment to activism, writing, and filmmaking, all aimed at engaging with and addressing broader societal issues. Through his efforts, Kareem has continued to embody the principles of hard work, integrity, and the pursuit of knowledge that defined his basketball career.

As an author, Kareem has penned several books that explore various facets of history, culture, and sports. His writings not only reflect his deep intellectual interests but also his desire to share knowledge and insights with others. Through his literary work, Kareem has provided valuable perspectives on important social and historical topics, further establishing his role as a thoughtful and influential public figure.

Kareem's dedication to social justice and equality has made him a respected voice in discussions on race, religion, and the role of athletes in activism. His willingness to speak out on these issues has inspired countless individuals, both within and outside the sports world, to engage with and work towards addressing societal challenges. Kareem's advocacy serves as a reminder that athletes have a powerful platform that can be used to effect positive change in the world.

Kareem's legacy is seen in the generations of players who have been influenced by his style of play, his work ethic, and his approach to the game. The skyhook, once Kareem's signature move, is remembered as one of the most iconic shots in basketball history, a symbol of both skill and innovation. Kareem's career serves as a benchmark for aspiring players, a shining example of how talent, when coupled with dedication and a constant desire to improve, can lead to unparalleled success.

Kareem's impact on basketball extends to his contributions to the development of the sport. Through coaching roles and mentorship, Kareem has imparted his knowledge and experience to younger players, helping to shape the future of basketball. His influence is evident in the way the game is played today, with an emphasis on skill, versatility, and basketball intelligence.

Kareem Abdul-Jabbar's legacy is multifaceted. In basketball, he is celebrated as one of the greatest players of all time. Beyond the game, Kareem is recognized as an intellectual, an activist, and a role model who has used his platform to advocate for meaningful change.

Chapter 5:
Lisa Leslie and the WNBA

∞

Towering above many, both in height and achievements, Lisa Leslie's journey through basketball is a captivating tale of determination, skill, and pioneering spirit. Her story isn't just about personal triumphs; it's about breaking new ground in women's sports and inspiring a generation of athletes to dream big. As a central figure in the Women's National Basketball Association (WNBA), Lisa's contributions have been instrumental in elevating the game to new heights.

From her early days in Gardena, California, Lisa's athletic prowess was evident. Basketball, however, was where her heart truly lay. Dominating the court in high school with her exceptional skills and height, Lisa quickly made a name for herself, hinting at the bright future that lay ahead in the sport she loved.

The journey from high school courts to the grand stages of college basketball saw Lisa's talents blossom even further. Attending the University of Southern California (USC), she became a beacon of excellence in women's college basketball. Her time at USC was marked by record-breaking performances and a slew of awards that celebrated her all-around capabilities on the court. Lisa was more than a player; she was a phenomenon in the making.

With the inception of the WNBA in 1997, a new chapter began not just for Lisa but for women's basketball in the United States. The league offered a platform like never before for female athletes to showcase their talent on a professional level. Lisa, with her stellar college career, was a natural fit for this new arena of competition. Drafted into the WNBA, she joined the Los Angeles Sparks, ready to make her mark in the professional world.

Lisa's impact on the WNBA was immediate and profound. On the court, she was a force to be reckoned with, known for her scoring, rebounding, and defensive skills. Her presence was not just about individual accolades; Lisa was a cornerstone for the Sparks, embodying leadership, teamwork, and a relentless pursuit of victory.

One of the defining moments of Lisa's career, and a landmark for the WNBA, was when she became the first woman to dunk in a professional game. This achievement transcended personal success; it was a statement about the evolving capabilities and competitive nature of women's basketball. Lisa Leslie, through moments like these, was not just setting records; she was reshaping the perception of women's sports.

Throughout her illustrious career in the WNBA, Lisa accumulated a wealth of honors, from MVP titles to championship victories. Each season, she pushed the boundaries of her abilities, striving for excellence and setting new standards for the league. Her dedication to the game and her role in promoting women's basketball have left an indelible impact on the sport.

Lisa's legacy, however, extends beyond the basketball court. As a mentor, role model, and advocate for women's sports, she has inspired countless young athletes to pursue their dreams with the same fervor and commitment she displayed throughout her career.

Lisa Leslie's journey through the ranks of women's basketball was punctuated by her unparalleled work ethic and a relentless drive to excel. Her transition from a promising high school talent to a collegiate superstar at USC set the stage for her groundbreaking career in the WNBA. At USC, Lisa didn't just play basketball; she embodied it, transforming every challenge into an opportunity to grow and every game into a chance to shine.

Her collegiate years were marked by spectacular performances, earning her accolades that spoke volumes of her dominance on the court. But for Lisa, the accolades were not the end goal; they were milestones on her journey to greatness. Her sights were set on a larger canvas—the burgeoning stage of the WNBA, where she would etch her name among the legends of the game.

Drafted by the Los Angeles Sparks, Lisa Leslie didn't just join a team; she became its cornerstone. From her very first season, Lisa's influence was unmistakable. She brought not only her scoring prowess and defensive skills but also a leadership quality that would become the backbone of the Sparks. Her ability to inspire her teammates, coupled with her own standout performances, quickly made her one of the most respected figures in the league.

Lisa's career in the WNBA was a series of groundbreaking achievements, each elevating the status of women's basketball. Her historic dunk, a feat never before accomplished in a WNBA game, shattered stereotypes and set a new benchmark for what female athletes could achieve. But Lisa's contributions weren't limited to scoring points. She was a defensive powerhouse, a leader in rebounds, and a critical player in the Sparks' championship victories.

Beyond her individual achievements, Lisa Leslie played a pivotal role in the growth and popularity of the WNBA. Her presence on the court drew fans and aspiring athletes to the games, showcasing the high level of competition and skill in women's basketball. Lisa was more than a player; she was an ambassador for the sport, advocating for greater recognition and support for women's basketball.

Off the court, Lisa's impact was equally profound. She was a role model for young girls, showing them that with hard work and determination, they could achieve their dreams. Her involvement in community service and her efforts to promote education and healthy living further exemplified her commitment to making a positive impact beyond basketball.

The challenges Lisa Leslie faced on her path to WNBA stardom were numerous, but her resilience and determination turned potential setbacks into stepping stones for success. Each obstacle she encountered, from intense competition to injuries, only served to strengthen her resolve and enhance her game. Lisa's ability to rise above adversity became one of her defining traits, endearing her to fans and solidifying her status as a leader on and off the court.

Lisa's influence extended beyond her physical presence in the game. She was a tactician, understanding the nuances of basketball at a level that allowed her to outthink opponents and make strategic plays that led to victories for the Los Angeles Sparks. Her basketball IQ was complemented by an unwavering spirit and a commitment to excellence that inspired her teammates to elevate their own performances. Under Lisa's leadership, the Sparks achieved remarkable success, including multiple WNBA championships that cemented their place in the league's history.

But Lisa Leslie's legacy is not confined to the records she set or the titles she won. Her impact on the WNBA and women's basketball as a whole is profound and multifaceted. She played a crucial role in increasing the visibility of the league, drawing attention to the skill, athleticism, and competitiveness of women's basketball. Lisa's success challenged perceptions and expanded the fan base for women's basketball, contributing to the sport's growing popularity and respect on a global scale.

Moreover, Lisa's commitment to mentorship and development had a lasting effect on the next generation of players. She was generous with her knowledge, offering guidance and support to younger athletes and helping to foster a culture of excellence and camaraderie within the WNBA. Her influence helped shape the careers of many players, ensuring the continued growth and success of the league.

Off the court, Lisa Leslie's contributions to society reflect her diverse interests and her desire to make a positive impact in the world. From her involvement in charitable causes to her advocacy for women's rights and empowerment, Lisa has used her platform to champion important issues. Her endeavors outside of basketball, including her role as a sports analyst, author, and speaker, showcase her multifaceted talents and her commitment to inspiring others to achieve their best.

As we reflect on Lisa Leslie's remarkable career and the legacy she has built, it's clear that her contributions extend far beyond the basketball court. She has left an indelible mark on the WNBA, on women's sports, and on the countless individuals she has inspired through her actions and achievements. Lisa Leslie's story is one of triumph, leadership, and the enduring power of setting an example for others to follow.

The culmination of Lisa Leslie's illustrious career in the WNBA marked not an end, but the beginning of a lasting legacy that transcends the sport of basketball. As one of the pioneering figures in women's basketball, her impact is measured not just in points scored or championships won, but in the doors she has opened for future generations of female athletes. Lisa's journey is a beacon of inspiration, showcasing the heights that can be achieved through dedication, hard work, and an unwavering belief in one's abilities.

Lisa's retirement from professional basketball was a momentous occasion, celebrated not just by fans of the Los Angeles Sparks or the WNBA, but by the entire sports community. It was a recognition of a career that had fundamentally altered the landscape of women's basketball, elevating the game to unprecedented levels of popularity and respect. Her farewell from the court was a tribute to the indomitable spirit and the transformative impact she had on the sport she loved.

Beyond her tangible achievements, Lisa Leslie's influence continues to resonate within the WNBA and the broader world of sports. She laid the foundation for a more inclusive, competitive, and dynamic league, paving the way for the stars of today and tomorrow. The WNBA, thriving with talent and enjoying increasing support from fans and sponsors alike, is part of Lisa's legacy—a testament to her role in shaping the league's success and its bright future.

Lisa's contributions extend beyond the basketball court. Her work as a sports analyst, author, and advocate for women's rights keeps her at the forefront of discussions on sports, gender equality, and empowerment. Lisa Leslie has gracefully transitioned from a dominant player to a respected voice in the sports community, continuing to inspire and influence through her insights and advocacy.

For young girls picking up a basketball for the first time, Lisa Leslie's story is a source of motivation—a reminder that with passion and perseverance, the highest pinnacles of success are within reach. She has shown that athletes can be much more than just competitors; they can be leaders, role models, and agents of change.

Lisa's journey from a young girl with a dream to one of the most influential figures in women's basketball is a powerful narrative of achievement and impact. Her legacy is a guiding light for the WNBA, for aspiring athletes, and for anyone who believes in the transformative power of sports to shape lives and influence society positively. Lisa Leslie's story is a testament to the enduring impact of a trailblazer who changed the game forever.

Chapter 6:
Giannis Antetokounmpo: From Rags to Riches

∞

Giannis Antetokounmpo's story reads like a fairy tale, a journey from humble beginnings in Athens, Greece, to the dazzling heights of the NBA. Known as the "Greek Freak" for his incredible athleticism and versatility on the basketball court, Giannis's path to stardom is a testament to perseverance, hard work, and the unyielding belief in one's dreams.

Born to Nigerian immigrants in Greece, Giannis grew up in a neighborhood where opportunities were scarce, and the future seemed uncertain. His family faced numerous challenges, from financial struggles to the constant threat of deportation. Despite these hardships, Giannis and his brothers found solace and joy in the game of basketball, playing with a makeshift ball and dreaming of a better life.

Giannis's talent on the basketball court became apparent early on. Tall, agile, and with an unmatched work ethic, he soon caught the eye of local basketball coaches. However, Giannis's journey was fraught with obstacles. His family's financial situation meant that basketball shoes, proper training equipment, and even transportation to games and practices were luxuries they could hardly afford.

Despite these challenges, Giannis's passion for basketball never waned. He spent countless hours practicing, honing his skills on makeshift courts, and learning from every game he played. His dedication began to pay off as he made a name for himself in the local basketball leagues, his unique blend of height, skill, and determination setting him apart from his peers.

Giannis's big break came when he was offered a spot on a professional basketball team in Greece. This opportunity was a lifeline for Giannis and his family, offering a glimmer of hope and a chance for a better future. Playing professional basketball in Greece, Giannis showcased his incredible talent, captivating fans with his athleticism and basketball IQ.

His performances in Greece were just the beginning. Scouts from the NBA took notice of the young phenom, intrigued by his potential to become a star in the world's premier basketball league. In 2013, Giannis's dream became a reality when he was drafted into the NBA by the Milwaukee Bucks.

The transition to the NBA was not without its challenges. Giannis had to adapt to a new country, a new culture, and a level of competition unlike anything he had faced before. The early days were tough, with Giannis working tirelessly to improve his game and prove that he belonged among the best.

But Giannis's hard work, coupled with his natural talent, soon began to shine through. He quickly became a key player for the Bucks, known for his versatility, his ability to score, rebound, and assist, and his defensive prowess. Giannis's rise in the NBA was meteoric, with each season building on the last, propelling him to new heights and cementing his status as one of the league's top players.

Giannis Antetokounmpo's ascent in the NBA is a narrative rich with moments of triumph and testament to his indomitable spirit. Each season with the Milwaukee Bucks, Giannis expanded his skillset, transforming from a promising rookie into a dominant force in the league. His growth was not just in his physical prowess but also in his understanding of the game, showcasing a basketball IQ that belied his years.

The "Greek Freak," as Giannis came to be known, mesmerized fans with his electrifying plays, from soaring dunks to swift defensive blocks. His ability to play multiple positions and excel in each showcased a versatility rarely seen in the league. Giannis's unique blend of size, speed, and skill made him a matchup nightmare for opponents and a valuable asset for the Bucks.

Giannis's commitment to improvement was evident in his rigorous training regimen. He spent countless hours in the gym, working on everything from shooting to ball-handling, determined to eliminate any weaknesses in his game. This dedication to excellence was a hallmark of Giannis's career, earning him the respect of teammates, coaches, and opponents alike.

One of the most defining moments in Giannis's journey came when he was named the NBA's Most Valuable Player (MVP). This accolade was a recognition of his incredible contributions to the game and his team's success. Winning the MVP was a dream come true for Giannis, a validation of his hard work and a symbol of his rise to the upper echelons of the basketball world.

Giannis's impact on the court was matched by his influence off it. He became an inspiration to millions around the globe, a living example of how determination and hard work can overcome even the most daunting of obstacles. Giannis's story resonated particularly with young athletes, who saw in him a role model who had achieved greatness through perseverance and dedication.

Despite his success, Giannis remained humble and grounded, always remembering his roots and the journey that brought him to the pinnacle of basketball. He used his platform to give back, engaging in community service and charity work, and advocating for those less fortunate. Giannis's humility and generosity endeared him even more to fans and solidified his status as not just a great player but a great person.

As Giannis's career progressed, he continued to set new benchmarks and achieve new milestones, each adding another chapter to his incredible story. From winning MVP awards to leading the Bucks to deep playoff runs, Giannis's journey was a testament to the power of hard work, resilience, and the unwavering belief in one's dreams.

The challenges Giannis Antetokounmpo faced on his journey to NBA stardom were manifold, but each obstacle only served to strengthen his resolve and sharpen his focus. Adapting to the NBA's fast-paced and physically demanding style of play required Giannis to push the limits of his endurance and skill. Every game was a learning experience, a chance to grow and refine his abilities against some of the best athletes in the world.

Giannis's work ethic became legendary within the Bucks organization. His teammates often spoke of his dedication to improvement, his first-to-arrive and last-to-leave mentality that set the tone for the entire team. This relentless pursuit of excellence was not just about personal accolades for Giannis; it was about lifting his team and bringing success to the city of Milwaukee.

One of the most significant hurdles Giannis and the Bucks faced was translating regular-season success into playoff victories. The intensity of playoff basketball tested Giannis's leadership and resilience, challenging him to elevate his game when the stakes were highest. Each postseason brought its lessons, and Giannis absorbed them all, using each experience to come back stronger and more determined.

Giannis became a vocal presence in the locker room, encouraging his teammates, leading by example, and fostering a culture of unity and determination. His growth into a team leader was a natural progression, reflective of his understanding of the responsibility that came with his talents.

The pinnacle of Giannis's NBA journey came when he led the Milwaukee Bucks to an NBA Championship. This victory was the culmination of years of hard work, a shared dream realized for Giannis, his teammates, and the city of Milwaukee. The championship was a testament to Giannis's incredible talent and his unwavering belief in his team's ability to overcome any obstacle.

Off the court, Giannis's journey from Athens to the NBA became a source of inspiration for millions worldwide. His story resonated particularly with young athletes facing their own challenges, serving as a powerful reminder that greatness is achievable, regardless of one's starting point. Giannis's humble beginnings and his rise to the top of the basketball world illustrated the transformative power of sports and the universal appeal of a story rooted in hard work and perseverance.

Giannis's impact on basketball extends beyond his individual achievements and the success of the Milwaukee Bucks. He has become a global ambassador for the sport, using his platform to promote basketball and its values around the world. Giannis's journey is a testament to the unifying power of sports, a story that transcends cultural and geographical boundaries.

The legacy Giannis Antetokounmpo is crafting extends far beyond the basketball court, weaving into the fabric of communities and touching the hearts of fans across the globe. As Giannis continues to dominate in the NBA, his story—a narrative of relentless perseverance, humility, and indomitable spirit—serves as a beacon of inspiration for aspiring athletes and individuals from all walks of life.

Giannis's influence is palpable not only in the records he breaks or the games he wins but in the way he carries himself both on and off the court. His commitment to family, his gratitude for the opportunities he's been given, and his desire to give back to the community reflect the depth of his character. Giannis understands the platform he has been given and uses it to advocate for positive change, embodying the role of a modern-day sports hero who recognizes the power of his voice.

In Milwaukee and beyond, Giannis is celebrated not just for the joy he brings to the game of basketball but for his contributions to society. His initiatives, aimed at supporting children and families in need, underscore his understanding that true greatness is measured by one's ability to uplift others. Giannis's journey from rags to riches is not merely a personal triumph but a story of hope and empowerment, encouraging others to believe in the possibility of a brighter future.

As Giannis's career progresses, the impact of his journey continues to unfold. Each game is a testament to his growth as a player and a person, showcasing his evolution from a young talent to a leader who inspires through action. The legacy Giannis is building transcends championships and accolades; it is rooted in the indelible mark he leaves on the hearts of those who witness his journey and the countless individuals he inspires to pursue their dreams with unwavering determination.

Giannis's story will be remembered as one of the most compelling tales of determination, resilience, and success. From the streets of Athens to the pinnacle of the NBA, Giannis's journey is a powerful reminder that no dream is too big, and no obstacle is insurmountable with hard work, perseverance, and a heart full of dreams.

Chapter 7:
Stephen Curry's Three-Point Revolution

∞

Known for his incredible shooting skills, especially from beyond the three-point line, Stephen Curry has revolutionized the game of basketball, making the three-pointer a central part of the sport's strategy and excitement.

Stephen's journey began in Akron, Ohio, where he was born into a family that loved basketball. His father, Dell Curry, was a professional basketball player, and from a very young age, Stephen was immersed in the sport. But it wasn't just his family background that made Stephen a basketball prodigy; it was his dedication, hard work, and a unique approach to the game that set him apart.

As a kid, Stephen was not the tallest or the strongest player on the court, but he had a secret weapon: his shooting ability. He practiced for hours, perfecting his form and technique, and developing what would become the most lethal three-point shot in the history of basketball. Stephen's ability to shoot from long range, often well beyond the three-point line, would become his signature move, dazzling fans and confounding opponents.

Stephen's high school career was marked by impressive performances, but despite his talent, he was not heavily recruited by the top college basketball programs. They doubted his ability to compete at the highest level due to his slight build. Undeterred, Stephen accepted a scholarship from Davidson College, a smaller school where he would have the opportunity to prove his doubters wrong.

At Davidson, Stephen's star shone brighter than ever. He led his team to remarkable victories, including a memorable run in the NCAA tournament that captured the nation's attention. Stephen's incredible shooting, quick decision-making, and leadership on the court made him a college basketball sensation, setting the stage for his entry into the NBA.

Drafted by the Golden State Warriors, Stephen quickly made an impact in the league. His exceptional shooting range, accuracy, and ability to make shots under pressure transformed the Warriors' offense and changed the way the game was played. Teams across the NBA took notice, and soon, the three-point shot, once considered a risky move, became a staple in basketball strategy, thanks in large part to Stephen's influence.

Stephen's impact on the game goes beyond just his shooting ability. His unselfish play, vision on the court, and knack for making his teammates better have been key to the

Warriors' success. Under Stephen's leadership, the team has secured multiple NBA championships, establishing a dynasty in the modern era of basketball.

But Stephen's revolution isn't just about the trophies and records; it's about how he's inspired players at all levels to view the three-point shot as a powerful tool in their arsenal. Young players, from the playgrounds to high school gyms, dream of shooting like Stephen, practicing their three-pointers with hopes of emulating their hero.

Stephen Curry's ascent in the NBA wasn't just a personal triumph; it marked a seismic shift in basketball strategy and play. His ability to sink three-pointers from seemingly impossible distances forced teams to rethink their defensive approaches, extending their coverage far beyond the traditional perimeter. The basketball court, under Stephen's influence, became a place where long-range shots were not just attempted in desperation but celebrated as a key offensive strategy.

The "Splash Brothers," a nickname given to Stephen and his teammate Klay Thompson, became synonymous with this long-range barrage. Together, they shattered records for three-pointers made in a season, both as individuals and as a duo. Their synergy on the court was electrifying, turning Warriors' games into must-watch events for basketball fans around the world.

Stephen's prowess from beyond the arc was matched by his agility and creativity. He had a knack for dribbling past defenders with a mesmerizing blend of speed and precision, often finishing with a layup, a mid-range jumper, or a pass to an open teammate. This versatility made him unpredictable and difficult to defend, adding layers to the Warriors' offensive playbook.

One of Stephen's most remarkable seasons came when he became the first player in NBA history to be named the Most Valuable Player (MVP) by unanimous vote. This accolade was a testament to his extraordinary impact on the game, showcasing not just his scoring ability but his leadership, sportsmanship, and influence on the team's success.

Off the court, Stephen's dedication to his craft was evident in his training regimen. Known for his meticulous approach to practice, he worked tirelessly to refine his shot, often experimenting with new techniques to improve his accuracy and range. This commitment to excellence inspired his teammates and young players alike, setting a new standard for what it means to be a professional athlete.

Stephen's impact extended beyond the realm of professional basketball. He became a role model for aspiring athletes, embodying the values of hard work, humility, and perseverance. His basketball camps, aimed at young players, emphasized not just skill development but also the importance of character, education, and giving back to the community.

Stephen Curry's influence on basketball can be seen not just in the record books but in the very fabric of the game itself. His success with the three-pointer has inspired teams across the NBA and around the world to embrace this once-underutilized shot as a fundamental part of their offensive strategy. The game has become more dynamic and fast-paced, with players at every position now expected to be proficient from beyond the arc, all thanks to the trail blazed by Stephen.

But Stephen's impact is perhaps most palpable in the next generation of players. Young athletes, from grade school to college, idolize Curry and strive to mimic his playing style. They practice his signature deep threes and his adept ball-handling, dreaming of one day emulating his success. Stephen has made the three-pointer not just a skill to be learned but an art to be mastered, changing the aspirations of countless young basketball players.

Despite his transformative impact on the game, Stephen has remained grounded and focused. He's known for his humility and team-first attitude, often crediting his teammates and coaches for his success. This leadership style has fostered a strong sense of camaraderie and unity within the Warriors, contributing to their sustained success over the years.

Stephen's contributions off the court are equally impressive. Through his charitable foundation, he has worked tirelessly to give back to the community, focusing on education, youth sports, and health and wellness initiatives. Stephen's philanthropic efforts reflect his belief in using his platform for the greater good, further endearing him to fans and making him a true ambassador of the sport.

As Stephen Curry's career progresses, his legacy continues to evolve. Each game is an opportunity to set new records, inspire more fans, and push the boundaries of what's possible in basketball. His journey is a testament to the power of innovation, dedication, and the relentless pursuit of greatness.

The culmination of Stephen Curry's three-point revolution marks a pivotal chapter in the annals of basketball history. His journey from a doubted college player to a transformative figure in the NBA encapsulates the essence of perseverance, innovation, and the relentless pursuit of excellence. Stephen's impact on the game extends beyond the dazzle of his long-range shots; it lies in the way he has inspired a paradigm shift in basketball strategy, making the three-pointer an indispensable tool in a team's offensive arsenal.

Stephen's legacy is not confined to the records he has shattered or the championships he has won with the Golden State Warriors. It is also reflected in the way he has changed the game for future generations. Young players now look up to Stephen, emulating his playing style and aspiring to possess the same sharpshooting prowess that made him a legend. The playgrounds and gyms across the globe echo with the sounds of children practicing three-pointers, dreaming of becoming the next Stephen Curry.

Beyond the basketball court, Stephen's influence is felt in his humanitarian efforts and community engagement. His commitment to making a positive impact off the court, through education initiatives, support for underprivileged communities, and health and wellness programs, showcases the breadth of his legacy. Stephen Curry is not just a basketball icon; he is a role model who exemplifies the values of hard work, humility, and giving back.

As we close this chapter on Stephen Curry's three-point revolution, we are reminded that his story is a beacon of hope and inspiration. It teaches us that limitations can be transcended, conventions can be challenged, and with passion and perseverance, new heights of success can be achieved. Stephen's journey reiterates that in the pursuit of greatness, it's not just about changing the game; it's about inspiring others to believe that they, too, can leave an indelible mark on the world.

Stephen Curry's legacy will continue to influence the sport of basketball for years to come. His revolutionary approach to the three-pointer has not only earned him a place among the game's all-time greats but has also redefined what is possible in basketball. As the next generation of players takes to the court, inspired by Stephen's achievements, his impact on the game will live on, a testament to the enduring power of vision, innovation, and the courage to dream big.

Chapter 8:
LeBron James: Basketball's Boy Wonder

∞

Lebron James' journey in the world of basketball is a story of talent, hard work, and a relentless pursuit of greatness. From his early days as a young prodigy in Akron, Ohio, to becoming one of the most celebrated players in NBA history, LeBron's path has been nothing short of spectacular. Known for his incredible athleticism, basketball IQ, and leadership on and off the court, LeBron has left an indelible mark on the sport.

Growing up in Akron, LeBron faced many challenges, but basketball became his refuge and passion. Even as a youngster, his talent on the basketball court was undeniable. LeBron was not just another kid who loved basketball; he was a phenomenon, dominating youth leagues and showing a level of skill and understanding of the game that was rare for someone his age.

LeBron's high school career at St. Vincent-St. Mary High School was marked by extraordinary achievements. He led his team to three state championships in four years, earning national attention and accolades. LeBron's high school games were so popular that they had to be moved to larger venues to accommodate the crowds of fans eager to watch him play. His prowess on the court, combined with his charisma and sportsmanship, made him one of the most highly anticipated prospects in the history of basketball.

The leap from high school sensation to NBA superstar was seamless for LeBron. Drafted as the first overall pick by the Cleveland Cavaliers, he immediately proved that he belonged in the league. LeBron's rookie season was sensational, earning him the NBA Rookie of the Year award and setting the stage for a career filled with record-breaking performances and accolades.

LeBron's impact on the court is characterized by his versatility. He is a player who can excel in any position, known for his ability to score, rebound, and assist with equal prowess. But what truly sets LeBron apart is his basketball IQ; his understanding of the game allows him to make split-second decisions that can change the outcome of a game. LeBron's leadership and ability to elevate the play of his teammates have been key factors in his success and the success of the teams he has played for.

Throughout his career, LeBron has faced high expectations and intense scrutiny, but he has consistently risen to the challenge, showcasing his resilience and dedication to the game. His journey through the NBA, from the Cavaliers to the Miami Heat, back to the Cavaliers, and then to the Los Angeles Lakers, has been marked by memorable moments, from game-winning shots to dominant playoff performances.

LeBron's influence extends beyond the basketball court. He is a role model and a leader in the community, using his platform to advocate for education, social justice, and the welfare of underprivileged children. LeBron's philanthropic efforts, particularly through his LeBron James Family Foundation, have made a significant impact, exemplifying his commitment to giving back and making a difference.

LeBron James' journey through the NBA has been marked by a series of awe-inspiring performances and significant milestones that have solidified his status as one of basketball's all-time greats. With each season, LeBron has continued to evolve as a player, adapting his game to maximize his strengths and lead his teams to victory. His ability to excel in high-pressure situations and deliver clutch performances has earned him the nickname "King James," a testament to his dominance on the basketball court.

One of the most defining aspects of LeBron's career has been his pursuit of championships. His decision to join the Miami Heat in 2010, forming a dynamic trio with Dwyane Wade and Chris Bosh, was a pivotal moment in his quest for NBA titles. The Heat's success, including back-to-back championships, was a testament to LeBron's leadership and his ability to galvanize a team around a common goal. LeBron's time in Miami showcased his growth as a player and a leader, setting the stage for his return to Cleveland and subsequent championship victory in 2016.

LeBron's championship with the Cleveland Cavaliers was particularly poignant, fulfilling a promise to bring a title to his home state of Ohio. The Cavaliers' historic comeback from a 3-1 deficit in the NBA Finals against the Golden State Warriors was a highlight of LeBron's career, underscoring his resilience and determination to succeed against all odds. This victory was more than just a triumph in basketball; it was a moment of immense pride and joy for the city of Cleveland and a crowning achievement in LeBron's storied career.

Throughout his time in the NBA, LeBron has been known for his exceptional all-around game. He is a prolific scorer, a tenacious defender, a gifted passer, and a strong rebounder. His versatility allows him to impact the game in multiple ways, making him a valuable asset to any team. LeBron's basketball IQ and understanding of the game have also made him an effective leader on the court, capable of making strategic decisions that lead to success.

LeBron's influence extends beyond his individual accomplishments. He has been a mentor to younger players, sharing his knowledge and experience to help them develop their skills and understand the nuances of the game. LeBron's commitment to teamwork and his ability to elevate the play of those around him have been hallmarks of his career, contributing to his reputation as one of the greatest players in the history of the sport.

Off the court, LeBron's impact is equally significant. His philanthropic efforts, particularly in the area of education, have made a lasting difference in the lives of countless children and families. LeBron's I PROMISE School, a public school in his hometown of Akron, Ohio, is a testament to his dedication to giving back and supporting his community. Through his foundation and various initiatives, LeBron has shown a deep commitment to social justice, equality, and the betterment of society.

LeBron James' ability to maintain an elite level of performance throughout his career is a testament to his dedication to physical fitness and continuous improvement. His rigorous training regimen and attention to recovery have allowed him to navigate the demands of long NBA seasons and the physical toll of countless playoff battles. LeBron's commitment to his body and his craft is a key factor in his longevity and success in the league.

Beyond his physical attributes and basketball skills, LeBron's leadership qualities have been instrumental in his teams' successes. His ability to inspire and motivate his teammates, coupled with his strategic basketball mind, makes him a natural leader on and off the court. LeBron's presence elevates the confidence and performance of those around him, making his teams formidable contenders year after year.

LeBron's journey back to the Cleveland Cavaliers and the historic 2016 NBA Championship victory is a highlight of his career that encapsulates his impact on the game. That championship was more than just a personal triumph; it was a victory for his hometown and a fulfillment of a promise to bring a title to Cleveland. The emotional weight of that achievement, both for LeBron and the city of Cleveland, underscored the deep connection between athletes and their communities.

The next chapter in LeBron's storied career saw him join the Los Angeles Lakers, adding another exciting dimension to his legacy. With the Lakers, LeBron continued to defy expectations, leading the team to an NBA Championship in

2020. This victory not only added to his collection of titles but also solidified his place among the all-time greats who have donned the Lakers' purple and gold.

On February 7, 2023, LeBron accomplished a feat that will forever live in basketball history. He became basketball's all-time leading scorer, passing Kareem Abdul-Jabbar's previous record of 38,387 points. This achievement is a testament to LeBron's longevity and consistency as one of the NBA's greatest players of all time. Many experts believe that it may be a very long time until this record is ever surpassed.

Off the court, LeBron's influence continues to grow. His voice on social and political issues has resonated far beyond the basketball community, making him a prominent figure in national conversations about justice and equality. LeBron's willingness to use his platform to advocate for change speaks to his character and his understanding of the impact he can have as a public figure.

LeBron's philanthropic efforts, particularly through the LeBron James Family Foundation, have made a significant impact on education and youth development. His commitment to creating opportunities for underprivileged children highlights his belief in the power of education and his desire to give back to his community.

As we reflect on LeBron James' extraordinary contributions to basketball and society, it's clear that his legacy is multifaceted. From his awe-inspiring performances on the court to his leadership and activism off it, LeBron's impact is profound and enduring. His journey from a young talent in Akron to a global sports icon is a compelling story of hard work, perseverance, and the relentless pursuit of greatness.

LeBron James' career is not just a collection of spectacular highlights and championships; it's a narrative of evolution, resilience, and the relentless pursuit of greatness. His journey has been characterized by a constant drive to improve, adapt, and lead, whether on the familiar hardwood of an NBA court or in the broader arena of societal impact.

One of the most remarkable aspects of LeBron's legacy is his adaptability. Over the years, he has refined his game to meet the changing dynamics of professional basketball and the evolving needs of his teams. From developing a more reliable three-point shot to enhancing his post-up game, LeBron has demonstrated a willingness to evolve, ensuring his continued impact and relevance in the league.

LeBron's influence extends into the strategic realms of the game as well. Known for his high basketball IQ, he often plays a pivotal role in game planning and in-game adjustments, functioning almost as a coach on the floor. His ability to read the game and make decisive, strategic plays is a testament to his deep understanding of basketball and his commitment to team success.

Beyond individual accolades and team achievements, LeBron's impact on the NBA can be seen in the way he has helped shape the modern era of player empowerment. His decisions in free agency, his business acumen, and his advocacy for player rights have contributed to a shift in how athletes view their careers and their roles within the sports industry. LeBron has shown that players can be influential voices in discussions about league policies, team management, and social issues, setting a precedent for future generations.

Off the court, LeBron's endeavors in education, particularly through the establishment of the I PROMISE School in his hometown of Akron, Ohio, highlight his commitment to empowering young people. The school's innovative approach to education, focusing on holistic support for students and families, reflects LeBron's vision for making a lasting impact in his community. This initiative, among others, underscores his belief in the transformative power of education and his desire to provide opportunities for those who face challenges similar to those he encountered in his youth.

LeBron's involvement in various business ventures and media projects has also showcased his entrepreneurial spirit and his interest in leveraging his platform for creative and impactful endeavors. From producing content that highlights important social issues to investing in businesses that align with his values, LeBron has broadened the scope of what it means to be a professional athlete.

The legacy of LeBron James transcends the bounds of basketball courts and stat sheets, extending into the realms of leadership, philanthropy, and social activism. His journey from the streets of Akron to the zenith of global sports stardom is a testament to the profound impact an individual can have when talent is coupled with an unwavering commitment to personal growth and community upliftment.

LeBron's basketball prowess, characterized by his scoring ability, playmaking, and defensive skills, has been the foundation of his legendary status. However, it's his strategic mind, leadership, and ability to inspire his teammates that have truly set him apart. His championships across multiple teams highlight his role not just as a player but as a unifying force, bringing out the best in those around him and steering his teams to victory against the odds.

LeBron's philanthropic efforts, particularly the LeBron James Family Foundation and the I PROMISE School, underscore his commitment to giving back to his community and empowering the next generation. These initiatives reflect LeBron's understanding of his platform's power and his responsibility to use it for the greater good.

Further, LeBron's voice in social and political matters has made him a prominent figure in the ongoing dialogue around justice and equality. His willingness to speak out on critical issues, even in the face of criticism, demonstrates his dedication to leveraging his influence for societal change. LeBron's activism extends beyond statements, as he actively engages in initiatives that address systemic issues and promote positive change.

As LeBron continues to build on his illustrious career and add to his scoring record, his legacy evolves to encompass not just his basketball achievements but his contributions to society. His journey is a beacon for young athletes and individuals from all walks of life, illustrating that success is not measured by personal accolades alone but by the ability to positively impact the lives of others.

Chapter 9:
The Shot Heard 'Round the World: Jordan's Buzzer Beater in 1989

There are moments in sports that take our breath away and are cherished and remembered for years to come. One such unforgettable moment is Michael Jordan's iconic buzzer-beater in the 1989 NBA playoffs, a shot that has since been etched into the annals of basketball history as "The Shot." This incredible play not only showcased Jordan's unmatched skill and composure under pressure but also marked a defining moment in his illustrious career.

The stage was set on May 7, 1989, during a fiercely contested playoff game between the Chicago Bulls and the Cleveland Cavaliers. The series had been a back-and-forth battle, with both teams showcasing their talent and determination. But as the final seconds of Game 5 ticked away, the Bulls found themselves trailing by one point, their hopes of advancing in the playoffs hanging by a thread.

With just three seconds left on the clock, the Bulls had possession of the ball, and everyone in the arena knew who it was going to. Michael Jordan, already known for his clutch performances, was about to face one of the biggest tests of his career. The atmosphere was electric, the tension palpable, as fans and players alike held their breath in anticipation.

The play that unfolded would become one of the most replayed and celebrated moments in sports history. The Bulls executed a perfect inbounds play, getting the ball to Jordan. With the clock winding down, Jordan dribbled to the foul line, evading the defense with a quick move. Then, in what seemed like a moment frozen in time, Jordan leaped into the air, releasing the ball with his signature finesse just as the buzzer sounded.

The ball arced gracefully through the air, the entire arena watching in suspense. And then, as if destined to go in, the ball swished through the net, giving the Bulls a one-point victory and sending them through to the next round of the playoffs. The crowd erupted in a mix of disbelief and elation, while Jordan pumped his fist in triumph, having once again proven why he was considered one of the greatest to ever play the game.

"The Shot" was more than just a game-winning buzzer-beater; it was a testament to Jordan's incredible skill, his ability to perform under immense pressure, and his unwavering confidence in his own abilities. It was a moment that transcended the game of basketball, inspiring countless young players to dream big and work hard, hoping to one day emulate their hero's heroics.

The backdrop to "The Shot" was a season filled with incredible performances by Michael Jordan, who had already established himself as a force to be reckoned with in the NBA. The 1988-1989 season saw Jordan showcasing his all-around game, dominating not just as a scorer but as a playmaker, defender, and leader for the Chicago Bulls. His prowess on the court had elevated the Bulls to playoff contenders, setting the stage for the dramatic confrontation with the Cleveland Cavaliers.

The Cavaliers were a formidable opponent, boasting a talented roster and a strong desire to make their mark in the playoffs. The series between the Bulls and the Cavaliers was intensely competitive, with each game being a hard-fought battle. The rivalry was not just about advancing in the playoffs; it was a test of wills, a challenge to see which team could rise to the occasion under the immense pressure of postseason basketball.

As the series progressed to Game 5, the stakes could not have been higher. The game was a back-and-forth affair, with both teams exchanging leads and showcasing their determination to win. The intensity of the game reflected the passion and dedication of the players, each one aware of what was on the line. For the Bulls, and especially for Michael Jordan, the game was an opportunity to silence the doubters and prove that they were championship contenders.

With the game on the line and the Bulls trailing by one point in the final seconds, the tension in the arena was palpable. The Bulls needed a hero, and all eyes turned to

Michael Jordan. Jordan's reputation for delivering in clutch moments was well-known, and the anticipation for what he might do in those final seconds was electric.

The inbounds play that led to "The Shot" was a masterpiece of strategy and execution. The Bulls' coach, Doug Collins, designed a play that would give Jordan the best chance to score, knowing that the Cavaliers would be doing everything in their power to stop him. The Bulls' players executed the play flawlessly, setting screens and creating the space Jordan needed to receive the ball.

As Jordan caught the ball and began his move, time seemed to slow down. His dribble, the evasive maneuver to create separation from the defender, and the leap for the shot were all executed with a precision that spoke to Jordan's mastery of the game. The release of the ball, the arc of the shot, and the final buzzer created a moment of suspense that captivated everyone watching.

When the ball swished through the net, the reaction was immediate and overwhelming. The Bulls' bench erupted in celebration, the fans in the arena and watching at home were in awe, and Jordan's iconic fist pump captured the sheer joy and relief of the moment. "The Shot" was not just a game-winner; it was a declaration of Jordan's greatness and a moment that would be remembered forever in the annals of basketball history.

The ripple effects of "The Shot" extended far beyond the immediate aftermath of the game. In the days and weeks that followed, this incredible moment was replayed on television screens and discussed on radio shows across the country, capturing the imagination of basketball fans everywhere.

Michael Jordan's already rising star soared even higher, as "The Shot" became a defining moment in his career, a clear indication of his ability to perform under the most intense pressure.

For the Chicago Bulls, "The Shot" was more than just a spectacular end to a playoff game; it was a catalyst that propelled the team into the national spotlight. It marked the Bulls as serious contenders in the NBA, a team led by a player capable of turning the tide of a game with a single play. The confidence gained from such a dramatic victory had a lasting impact on the team, setting the tone for their approach to future challenges.

In the broader context of NBA history, "The Shot" highlighted the growing importance of individual heroics in basketball. It underscored the idea that a single player, with the right combination of skill, determination, and confidence, could change the outcome of a game, even a series. This concept resonated with players and coaches alike, influencing how teams approached game-winning situations and how young players aspired to develop their skills.

For young basketball fans watching at home, "The Shot" was a source of inspiration. It was a moment that spoke to the dreams of aspiring athletes, a demonstration of what was possible with hard work and belief in oneself. Michael Jordan became an even greater role model for countless kids who picked up a basketball, hoping to one day emulate his success and perhaps even replicate his iconic buzzer-beater.

The legacy of "The Shot" also extended to the Cleveland Cavaliers, the team on the losing end of that memorable play. For the Cavaliers and their fans, "The Shot" was a heart-wrenching moment, a reminder of how close they had come to advancing in the playoffs. However, it also served as a lesson in resilience, as the team and its supporters were forced to regroup and rebuild in the aftermath of such a dramatic loss.

As we reflect on the impact of "The Shot" and its place in basketball lore, it's clear that this moment was more than just a highlight in Michael Jordan's career. It was an event that captured the essence of competitive sports: the thrill of victory, the agony of defeat, and the enduring spirit of athletes who strive for greatness against all odds.

The enduring legacy of "The Shot" by Michael Jordan in the 1989 NBA playoffs transcends its immediate impact on the game, becoming a symbol of excellence, determination, and the sheer will to succeed. This iconic moment has been etched into the collective memory of basketball fans and players alike, serving as a source of inspiration and a benchmark for clutch performance in the sport.

For Michael Jordan, "The Shot" was one of many remarkable achievements in his storied career, yet it stands out for its dramatic nature and its timing in a high-stakes playoff game. It exemplified Jordan's ability to rise to the occasion when it mattered most, reinforcing his reputation as one of the greatest, if not the greatest, basketball players of all time. This singular play contributed to the mythos surrounding Jordan, a narrative built on moments of brilliance that defined his legacy.

In the broader context of the NBA, "The Shot" highlighted the importance of individual brilliance within the framework of a team sport. It demonstrated how one player's skill and confidence could sway the fate of a game, influencing coaching strategies and player development for years to come. The emphasis on developing the ability to take and make critical shots under pressure became a focal point for players aspiring to reach the heights of the sport.

For aspiring young athletes, "The Shot" has served as a powerful reminder that no moment is too big and that with hard work, confidence, and a never-say-die attitude, they too can achieve greatness. Jordan's legacy, punctuated by moments like "The Shot," continues to motivate and inspire future generations to dream big and pursue their goals with relentless determination.

Beyond the realm of basketball, "The Shot" has become a cultural touchstone, a reference point for excellence and clutch performance in various fields. It represents the idea that success is within reach, even in the face of seemingly insurmountable odds, if one is prepared to seize the moment with both hands.

Chapter 10:
Larry Bird, Magic Johnson, and the Celtics-Lakers Rivalry

∞

Few stories in basketball history are as captivating and enduring as the rivalry between Larry Bird of the Boston Celtics and Magic Johnson of the Los Angeles Lakers. This legendary matchup not only defined a golden era of the NBA but also transformed basketball into a global spectacle, captivating fans with their contrasting styles, mutual respect, and fierce competition.

Larry Bird, hailing from the small town of French Lick, Indiana, brought a blue-collar work ethic and a sharpshooting precision to the game. Known for his incredible basketball IQ, clutch shooting, and tenacious rebounding, Bird epitomized the Celtics' ethos of teamwork, grit, and determination. His arrival in Boston sparked a resurgence for the storied franchise, rekindling its championship aspirations.

On the opposite coast, Earvin "Magic" Johnson brought showmanship and unparalleled versatility to the Los Angeles Lakers. With his charismatic smile and exceptional playmaking skills, Magic was the perfect leader for the Lakers' fast-paced, glamorous style of play, known as "Showtime." His ability to play all five positions on the court and his infectious enthusiasm for the game made him a fan favorite and a nightmare for opponents.

The Bird-Magic rivalry officially began in college when Bird's Indiana State Sycamores faced off against Magic's Michigan State Spartans in the 1979 NCAA Championship game. Magic's team emerged victorious, setting the stage for a rivalry that would captivate the basketball world for the next decade. Both players entered the NBA later that year, with Bird joining the Celtics and Magic being drafted by the Lakers, reigniting the historic Celtics-Lakers rivalry that dated back to the 1950s.

Throughout the 1980s, Bird and Magic dominated the NBA, their teams meeting in the Finals three times. Each matchup was a clash of titans, with the Celtics' disciplined, team-oriented basketball pitted against the Lakers' fast-paced, electrifying style. The games were intense, often coming down to the wire, and showcased the incredible talents of both Bird and Magic.

The rivalry between Bird and Magic was about more than just wins and losses; it was a battle of ideals, a contrast of basketball philosophies, and a duel between two of the game's greatest minds. Despite their fierce competition on the court, Bird and Magic shared a deep mutual respect and a friendship that grew stronger over the years. Their sportsmanship and admiration for each other's talents were testaments to the character of both men.

Bird and Magic's rivalry brought unprecedented attention to the NBA, elevating the league's profile and turning basketball into a prime-time spectacle. Their battles were not just sports events; they were cultural moments that transcended the game, drawing in fans from around the world and inspiring a new generation of players.

The Celtics-Lakers rivalry, epitomized by the clashes between Larry Bird and Magic Johnson, was more than a series of basketball games; it was a saga that captured the essence of competition, excellence, and sportsmanship. Each encounter between these two teams during the 1980s was a masterclass in basketball, showcasing not only the individual brilliance of Bird and Magic but also the depth and talent of their respective teams.

Larry Bird, with his sharp eye for the game, was a strategist on the court. Known for his incredible shooting ability, he could make baskets from anywhere, often in the most clutch moments, earning him the nickname "Larry Legend." But Bird's contributions went beyond scoring; his rebounding, defense, and uncanny ability to make his teammates better were integral to the Celtics' success. Bird's leadership style was quiet yet commanding, inspiring his team through his tireless work ethic and commitment to winning.

On the other side, Magic Johnson was the embodiment of charisma and versatility. His exceptional passing and court vision revolutionized the point guard position, making him one of the most exciting players to watch. Magic's ability to elevate the play of his teammates was unparalleled, and his joy for the game was infectious. Under Magic's leadership, the Lakers' "Showtime" basketball became a symbol of the glitz and glamour of Los Angeles, attracting celebrities and fans alike to the Forum to witness the spectacle.

The Celtics and Lakers met in the NBA Finals three times during the 1980s, in 1984, 1985, and 1987, with each series contributing to the lore of the rivalry. The 1984 Finals saw the Celtics emerge victorious in a grueling seven-game series, reinforcing the team's resilience and toughness. The following year, the Lakers claimed the championship, becoming the first visiting team to win a title on the Celtics' home court, a victory that was particularly sweet for Magic, who had faced criticism for his performance in the previous year's Finals.

The 1987 Finals was another epic showdown, highlighted by Magic's iconic "baby sky hook" shot in Game 4, which clinched a crucial win for the Lakers. This series solidified the Lakers' dominance in the 1980s and marked another chapter in the storied rivalry between Bird and Magic.

Beyond their battles on the court, Bird and Magic's rivalry was characterized by a deep mutual respect and an unlikely friendship that developed over the years. Their competitive fire pushed each other to greatness, but off the court, they shared a bond that transcended the game. This relationship was beautifully captured in the 1992 Barcelona Olympics, where Bird and Magic, as teammates on the "Dream Team," won gold medals together, celebrating the culmination of their legendary careers.

The Celtics-Lakers rivalry, fueled by the epic confrontations between Larry Bird and Magic Johnson, did more than just entertain; it elevated the entire sport of basketball to new heights. The intense matchups between these two teams during the 1980s were not just games; they were compelling narratives that captivated audiences worldwide, drawing in fans who might never have otherwise watched basketball. This golden era of the NBA was marked by an increase in national television coverage, bringing the excitement of Bird vs. Magic into living rooms across America and beyond.

Bird and Magic's rivalry was a study in contrasts, not just in their playing styles but also in their personalities and the cities they represented. Larry Bird, with his stoic demeanor and fundamentally sound game, was the perfect embodiment of Boston's blue-collar, team-first basketball ethos. Meanwhile, Magic Johnson's infectious smile, flashy play, and magnetic personality mirrored the glitz and glamour of Los Angeles. This juxtaposition added an extra layer of intrigue to their encounters, making each game feel like a clash of basketball philosophies and cultures.

Despite their differences, Bird and Magic shared an unwavering commitment to excellence and a deep love for the game of basketball. Their rivalry pushed them to their limits, demanding the best of each other and their teammates. The intense competition brought out legendary performances, unforgettable moments, and a level of play that has become the benchmark for greatness in the NBA.

The impact of their rivalry extended beyond the court, influencing a generation of players who grew up watching Bird and Magic duel. Young athletes learned the value of hard work, dedication, and the importance of a strong competitive spirit from these two icons. The legacy of Bird and Magic's rivalry can be seen in the way the game is played today, with an emphasis on versatility, basketball IQ, and the importance of elevating the play of one's teammates.

Beyond basketball, Bird and Magic's relationship evolved from fierce competitors to lifelong friends. Their mutual respect and admiration for each other's talents and accomplishments only grew stronger with time. This friendship was beautifully showcased in their joint autobiography, "When the Game Was Ours," which provided an intimate look into their rivalry, careers, and the bond that formed between them. Their story is a testament to the power of sports to bring people together, transcending rivalries and competition.

The Celtics-Lakers rivalry, fueled by the extraordinary talents of Larry Bird and Magic Johnson, transcended the boundaries of the basketball court to become a cultural phenomenon. Their battles were not just about which team would emerge victorious; they were about contrasting styles, coasts, and philosophies, all embodied by these two basketball giants. This rivalry was a narrative that captivated not just hardcore basketball fans but also casual observers, drawing many into the fold of NBA fandom.

The media played a significant role in elevating the Bird-Magic rivalry to legendary status. The compelling narrative of the "Hick from French Lick" versus the charismatic star from Michigan State, representing two of the most storied franchises in NBA history, was irresistible. Television broadcasts, sports magazines, and newspapers all contributed to the hype, making each Celtics-Lakers game a must-watch event. The rivalry was not just about basketball; it was a story that captured the imagination of the nation.

The impact of Bird and Magic's rivalry on the NBA was profound. The league, which had struggled with image issues and financial instability in the years before their arrival, saw a resurgence in popularity and commercial success. Bird and Magic's duels brought a new level of excitement and competitiveness to the game, helping to lay the foundation for the global popularity of the NBA that would follow in the years to come.

Their rivalry also brought about a change in how basketball was played and perceived. Bird and Magic's all-around skills and high basketball IQ highlighted the importance of versatility and team play. They were not just scorers; they were leaders who made everyone around them better, emphasizing the value of assists, rebounds, and defensive plays just as much as points scored. This holistic approach to the game influenced generations of players who followed, shifting the focus from individual prowess to team dynamics and cooperation.

The legacy of the Larry Bird and Magic Johnson rivalry, emblematic of the Celtics-Lakers historical clash, transcends the confines of the 1980s or the basketball court itself. It's a narrative that has become integral to the fabric of the NBA, embodying the pinnacle of competitive spirit, athletic excellence, and the profound impact of sportsmanship.

Bird and Magic didn't just elevate their teams; they elevated the entire league, setting new standards for what it meant to be a professional athlete. Their rivalry was a masterclass in how to compete fiercely while maintaining respect for one's opponent. This lesson in sportsmanship has been passed down through generations, influencing how players approach the game and each other.

The influence of Bird and Magic's rivalry is also evident in the evolution of player relationships within the NBA. In an era where fierce competitors on the court can be close friends off it, the foundation of such dynamics can be traced back to the camaraderie that developed between these two legends. Their ability to balance intense rivalry with mutual respect and friendship paved the way for a new culture within the league, one where athletes can push each other to greatness while fostering personal connections.

Chapter 11:
Texas Western's 1966 NCAA Civil Rights Milestone

∞

In the history of basketball, few moments are as significant and transformative as the victory of the Texas Western College (now known as the University of Texas at El Paso, UTEP) basketball team in the 1966 NCAA Championship. This remarkable event wasn't just about winning a title; it was a pivotal moment in the civil rights movement, challenging racial barriers and changing the landscape of college basketball forever.

The story begins in the mid-1960s, a time when the United States was grappling with deep-seated racial tensions and the fight for civil rights was at its peak. In this era, college basketball, like many other aspects of society, was largely segregated, with few African American players on predominantly white teams, especially in the South.

Enter Don Haskins, the head coach of the Texas Western Miners. Haskins was a visionary who believed in talent and character over skin color. In a bold move, he recruited some of the best African American players from across the country, assembling a team that was talented, determined, and diverse. This decision was revolutionary at the time and set the stage for a historic season.

The Miners' journey to the 1966 NCAA Championship was nothing short of spectacular. With a combination of skill, teamwork, and sheer determination, they defied the odds, beating heavily favored teams and advancing to the national championship game against the University of Kentucky Wildcats, a team that epitomized the all-white powerhouse programs of the era.

The championship game, held on March 19, 1966, was more than just a battle for the title; it was a clash of ideologies, a confrontation between the old guard and a new, more inclusive vision of what college basketball could be. Coach Haskins made a groundbreaking decision to start five African American players – the first time this had ever been done in an NCAA Championship game.

The game was intense, with both teams showcasing their talent and drive. But it was the Miners' unity, their unshakable belief in each other, and their skill on the court that ultimately led them to victory. The image of the Texas Western team, jubilant in their triumph, became an iconic symbol of progress and a beacon of hope for a more inclusive and equitable future in sports and society.

Texas Western's victory in the 1966 NCAA Championship was a watershed moment that transcended sports. It challenged the status quo, broke down racial barriers, and paved the way for the integration of college athletics across the nation. The Miners' win was a testament to the power of sports as a catalyst for social change, proving that talent knows no color and that unity and diversity can lead to unprecedented success.

The Texas Western Miners' path to the 1966 NCAA Championship was not just a series of basketball games; it was a journey that challenged societal norms and pushed against the boundaries of segregation that had long defined American sports. Coach Don Haskins' decision to recruit talented African American players was a bold move in an era when such actions were met with resistance and, often, outright hostility.

As the Miners progressed through the season, their success on the court began to draw national attention. With each victory, they were not only inching closer to the championship but also making a statement about the importance of diversity and inclusion. The team's unity and camaraderie were evident to all who watched them play, showcasing the power of sports to bring people together, regardless of their background or skin color.

The Miners' diverse roster faced numerous challenges throughout the season, from hostile crowds to discriminatory practices in certain venues. Yet, they persevered, buoyed by their shared goal and the leadership of Coach Haskins, who remained steadfast in his belief in his players and his vision for the team. This resolve was a testament to the character of the team and their coach, who were not just playing for a title but for a cause much greater than themselves.

The climactic championship game against the Kentucky Wildcats, a team that epitomized the all-white basketball programs of the time, was more than just a contest of skill; it was a symbolic battle against the racial divides that plagued the nation. The Miners, with their starting lineup of five African American players, were not just representing Texas Western College; they were representing hope for a future where a person's worth was not judged by the color of their skin but by their talent, character, and hard work.

The victory of the Texas Western Miners in the 1966 NCAA Championship was a moment of triumph that resonated far beyond the basketball court. It sent shockwaves through the world of college sports and beyond, challenging long-held beliefs and opening doors for countless African American athletes who followed. The win was a validation of Coach Haskins' approach and a clear message that diversity and inclusion could lead to unparalleled success.

The impact of Texas Western's championship win was felt immediately, with colleges and universities across the nation beginning to actively recruit African American athletes, leading to the gradual integration of sports programs. This shift not only changed the face of college basketball but also contributed to the broader civil rights movement, highlighting the role of sports as a catalyst for social change.

The aftermath of Texas Western's groundbreaking victory in the 1966 NCAA Championship extended far beyond the realm of college basketball, leaving an indelible mark on the civil rights movement and setting a precedent for the integration of sports across the United States. The Miners' triumph was not just celebrated by basketball fans but hailed as a significant milestone in the fight for equality and justice.

The media played a crucial role in highlighting the significance of Texas Western's victory, with newspapers, magazines, and television broadcasts across the country covering the historic event. The story of a small college team breaking racial barriers to win the national championship captivated the nation, bringing attention to the ongoing struggles for civil rights and the potential for sports to serve as a unifying force.

In the years following their championship win, the Texas Western Miners were recognized and honored for their contributions to basketball and society. The team's story was shared in books, documentaries, and films, ensuring that the legacy of their achievement and the lessons learned from their journey continued to inspire and educate future generations.

The impact of Texas Western's victory was felt most acutely in the world of college athletics, where the integration of sports teams gained momentum. Universities that had previously resisted recruiting African American athletes began to recognize the value of diversity, both on the court and within the campus community. The success of the Miners demonstrated that talent and teamwork know no racial boundaries, leading to more inclusive and competitive sports programs nationwide.

The Miners' championship win challenged stereotypes and preconceptions about African American athletes, contributing to a broader societal shift in attitudes towards race and equality. By excelling in a high-pressure, highly visible environment, the Texas Western team proved that determination, skill, and character are the true measures of an athlete's worth, regardless of their background.

The legacy of the 1966 Texas Western Miners continues to resonate in the world of sports and beyond. Their story is a testament to the power of courage, conviction, and the pursuit of excellence. It serves as a reminder of the transformative impact that a group of determined individuals can have, not just in breaking down barriers in sports but in advancing the cause of civil rights and social justice.

The enduring influence of the Texas Western Miners' 1966 championship victory is a beacon for the transformative power of sports in society. This monumental event not only reshaped college basketball but also reinforced the role of athletics as a platform for social change. The Miners' triumph over adversity and discrimination serves as a compelling chapter in the broader narrative of the civil rights movement, illustrating how courage and solidarity can challenge and dismantle the barriers of segregation and prejudice.

In the years that followed their historic win, the Texas Western Miners were celebrated not just as champions on the court but as pioneers for equality and justice. Their legacy was immortalized in various forms, from commemorative events and museum exhibits to educational curriculums, ensuring that the significance of their achievement and the values they stood for would continue to resonate with future generations.

The story of the 1966 Miners also sparked conversations about representation and diversity in sports, highlighting the importance of providing equal opportunities for athletes of all backgrounds. This narrative contributed to a gradual but significant shift in attitudes towards race and inclusion within the sporting community and beyond, encouraging a more open and diverse environment in collegiate and professional sports.

The legacy of the Texas Western Miners and their historic championship win is a reminder of the potential for greatness that lies in unity, diversity, and the shared commitment to equality. Their journey from underdogs to champions, in the face of formidable challenges, continues to inspire and teach us the value of resilience, the importance of breaking down barriers, and the enduring power of believing in a cause greater than oneself.

Chapter 12:
The Triumph of the "Dream Team"

In the summer of 1992, something magical happened in the world of basketball that would forever change the international landscape of the sport. For the first time in Olympic history, professional NBA players were allowed to participate, leading to the formation of the "Dream Team." This team wasn't just any group of players; it was a once-in-a-lifetime assembly of the greatest basketball talents the world had ever seen, ready to represent the United States in the Barcelona Olympics.

The Dream Team boasted an incredible lineup, including legends like Michael Jordan, Magic Johnson, Larry Bird, and Charles Barkley, among others. Each member was a superstar in his own right, with numerous NBA championships, MVP awards, and All-Star appearances between them. The anticipation and excitement around this team were unparalleled, as fans around the globe eagerly awaited the chance to see these legends play together.

From the moment the Dream Team was announced, it was clear that they were not just aiming for gold; they were on a mission to showcase the beauty of basketball, to play the game at its highest level, and to inspire people everywhere with their skill, teamwork, and sportsmanship. The team's blend of talent, charisma, and competitive spirit made them not just athletes but ambassadors of the sport.

As the Olympics began, the Dream Team's impact was immediate and profound. They captivated audiences with their electrifying play, combining dazzling athleticism with precise execution and unselfish teamwork. Their games were more than just competitions; they were exhibitions of basketball artistry, with each pass, dunk, and three-pointer bringing fans to their feet.

The Dream Team's dominance on the court was unmatched. They won games by wide margins, but what stood out was the way they played the game. They displayed a joy and passion for basketball that was infectious, making each game a celebration of the sport. Their respect for their opponents and for the game itself was evident in every handshake, every smile, and every moment of camaraderie on and off the court.

The Dream Team's journey through the Olympics was a testament to the universal appeal of basketball. They brought together fans from all corners of the globe, uniting people through their love of the game. Their performances were a powerful reminder of the ability of sports to bridge cultural and linguistic divides, to create shared moments of joy and admiration.

The Dream Team's roster was like a who's who of basketball legends, each player bringing his unique talents and personality to the mix, creating an ensemble that was as formidable as it was mesmerizing to watch. Alongside Michael Jordan, Magic Johnson, and Larry Bird, the team included other stars whose contributions were pivotal to the Dream Team's success and allure.

Charles Barkley, with his larger-than-life personality and unmatched prowess on the court, was a force to be reckoned with. His ability to score, rebound, and ignite the team with his energy made him a standout player throughout the Olympics. Barkley's performances were not just effective; they were filled with the kind of flair and passion that made every game memorable.

Then there was Karl Malone, known as "The Mailman" because he always delivered. Malone's strength, scoring ability, and work ethic were crucial to the team's inside game. Paired with his Utah Jazz teammate John Stockton, one of the greatest point guards in NBA history, they brought a level of chemistry and precision to the Dream Team's play that was unparalleled. Stockton's vision and passing ability ensured that the ball always found its way to the right person at the right time, making the team's offense nearly unstoppable.

Patrick Ewing and David Robinson provided an imposing presence in the paint, altering shots, grabbing rebounds, and finishing strong at the rim. Their defensive prowess was a key component of the Dream Team's strategy, giving them the ability to shut down opponents and spark fast breaks that thrilled the crowds.

Scottie Pippen and Clyde Drexler brought athleticism and versatility to the team, able to play multiple positions and contribute in every aspect of the game. Their defensive skills, particularly Pippen's, were instrumental in setting the tone for the team, allowing the Dream Team to transition quickly from defense to offense and capitalize on their speed and agility.

Chris Mullin, with his sharpshooting ability, was another vital asset to the team. Mullin's precision from beyond the arc stretched opposing defenses and created space for his teammates to operate. His calm demeanor and professionalism added a steadying influence to the team's dynamic roster.

The Dream Team was coached by Chuck Daly, who managed to blend these towering egos and talents into a cohesive unit that played selflessly and joyfully. Daly's coaching philosophy emphasized the team's collective strength over individual accolades, a principle that guided the Dream Team to their Olympic success.

The Dream Team's journey through the 1992 Barcelona Olympics was marked by a series of unforgettable moments that showcased not only their unparalleled skill but also the spirit of camaraderie and sportsmanship that defined them. Each game was an opportunity for the players to demonstrate why they were considered the best in the world, and they did so with a style and grace that captivated audiences worldwide.

One of the most memorable aspects of the Dream Team's play was their incredible passing and teamwork. Despite being composed of individuals who were used to leading their respective NBA teams, the players adapted to their roles, focusing on the collective success of the team. The sight of Magic Johnson dishing out no-look passes, John Stockton orchestrating the offense with precision, and Michael Jordan and Scottie Pippen turning defense into art form, highlighted the team's commitment to playing beautiful basketball.

The Dream Team's dominance was such that they often found themselves leading by wide margins, allowing Coach Chuck Daly to give ample playing time to all members of the squad. This not only showcased the depth of talent on the team but also allowed players like Chris Mullin and Clyde Drexler to shine, hitting three-pointers and driving to the basket with the same ease and confidence as their more celebrated teammates.

Off the court, the Dream Team was a spectacle in itself. The players were treated like rock stars, with fans flocking to see them wherever they went. The camaraderie among the team members was evident, as they shared laughs, exchanged stories, and enjoyed the unique experience of representing their country together. This bond was particularly special for players like Larry Bird and Magic Johnson, who had transitioned from fierce NBA rivals to Olympic teammates, showcasing the unifying power of the Dream Team.

Despite their celebrity status and the ease with which they won games, the Dream Team remained focused on their mission – to showcase the best of American basketball and to reclaim the Olympic gold medal. Their respect for the game and their opponents was evident in every play, every handshake, and every interaction, earning them admiration not just for their talent but for their character.

As the Dream Team marched towards the gold medal, their impact on the sport of basketball became increasingly clear. They were not just winning games; they were inspiring a generation of players around the world, demonstrating the heights that could be achieved with hard work, talent, and teamwork. The global popularity of basketball surged in the wake of the Dream Team's triumph, with more and more international players aspiring to reach the NBA and follow in the footsteps of their Olympic heroes.

The climax of the Dream Team's journey at the 1992 Barcelona Olympics was the gold medal game, a match that was more a coronation than a contest. The Dream Team faced Croatia, a team led by talented players like Dražen Petrović and Toni Kukoč, who would later make their mark in the NBA. However, the outcome of the game seemed almost a foregone conclusion, given the sheer dominance the Dream Team had exhibited throughout the tournament.

The gold medal game was a display of basketball excellence. The Dream Team played with a mix of joy and precision, showcasing their individual talents while never losing sight of the team ethos that had brought them together. Every player contributed to the victory, and when the final buzzer sounded, the score reflected the Dream Team's supremacy in the tournament. The United States had reclaimed its position atop the basketball world, and the players celebrated together, basking in the glory of their achievement.

The victory was more than just a triumph in sports; it was a moment of cultural significance. The Dream Team had not only won the gold medal but had also won the hearts of fans around the world. They had shown that basketball was more than a game; it was a unifying force, capable of transcending borders and bringing together people from different backgrounds and cultures.

The Dream Team set a new standard for international basketball, raising the bar for what was expected of Olympic teams. Their influence was felt in the years that followed, as more international players entered the NBA, enriching the league with their diverse skills and perspectives. Basketball became a truly global sport, with the Dream Team's influence reaching far beyond the United States.

The players themselves became ambassadors for basketball, recognized and revered wherever they went. Their time together as the Dream Team was a defining moment in each of their careers, a shared experience that they would carry with them long after their playing days were over.

The Dream Team was a testament to the power of collective talent, the joy of competition, and the beauty of sport as a platform for unity and inspiration. Their story is a reminder of the incredible achievements that are possible when individuals come together, united by a common goal and a shared love for the game of basketball.

Chapter 13:
The Harlem Globetrotters

∞

The Harlem Globetrotters hold a special place in the story of basketball, weaving together athleticism, entertainment, and a pioneering spirit that has captivated audiences worldwide for decades. This remarkable team, known for their incredible basketball skills and hilarious on-court antics, has not only brought joy and laughter to millions but has also played a significant role in breaking down racial barriers in sports.

The story of the Harlem Globetrotters begins in the 1920s, but not in Harlem, New York, as their name might suggest. Instead, the team originated in the South Side of Chicago, Illinois, where a group of African American basketball players decided to form a team. Their early games were played in the Chicago area, but it wasn't long before they took their show on the road, traveling across the United States to showcase their talents.

The name "Harlem Globetrotters" was adopted as a nod to Harlem's reputation as the center of African American culture and also to give the impression that the team had traveled the world, even though their early tours were confined to the U.S. The "Globetrotters" part of their name reflected the team's ambition to take their game international, a goal they would achieve with great success in the years to come.

What set the Harlem Globetrotters apart was their unique blend of exceptional basketball skill and comedic entertainment. They were masters of the game, known for their impressive dribbling, shooting, and passing abilities. But they added a twist to their performances, incorporating slapstick comedy, theatrical skits, and audience interaction into their games. This combination of sports and entertainment made Globetrotters' games unlike any other basketball event, appealing to fans of all ages and backgrounds.

The team's roster over the years has included some of the most talented and charismatic players in the game. One of the most famous Globetrotters was Meadowlark Lemon, known as the "Clown Prince of Basketball." His incredible skills and infectious humor made him a fan favorite and epitomized the spirit of the Globetrotters. Another standout was Curly Neal, whose bald head and exceptional ball-handling skills became iconic symbols of the team.

As the Harlem Globetrotters traveled the world, they became ambassadors of basketball and goodwill. Their tours took them to distant lands, where they often became the first Americans, let alone African American athletes, that local populations had ever seen. Through their games, the

Globetrotters introduced the sport of basketball to international audiences, spreading the love for the game across the globe.

In an era when racial segregation and discrimination were rampant in the United States, the Globetrotters broke down barriers, playing in front of integrated audiences and challenging stereotypes about African American athletes. Their success and popularity played a part in paving the way for the integration of professional sports leagues.

The Harlem Globetrotters' journey through the decades is a testament to their enduring appeal and the universal language of basketball. As they crisscrossed the globe, the Globetrotters not only showcased their incredible basketball skills but also bridged cultural gaps, bringing smiles and laughter to people from all walks of life. Their performances were more than just basketball games; they were a celebration of joy, creativity, and the human spirit.

One of the most remarkable aspects of the Globetrotters' performances was their ability to innovate and keep their routines fresh and exciting. From their signature "Magic Circle" warm-up, where players showcased their individual ball-handling and trick-shot skills, to the game's playful interactions with referees and opponents, the Globetrotters continuously found new ways to entertain and amaze their audiences.

The team's impact on the sport of basketball cannot be overstated. The Globetrotters were pioneers in popularizing the game internationally, long before global broadcasts and the internet made NBA games accessible worldwide. Their tours introduced basketball to countless countries, laying the groundwork for the sport's global popularity today. In many ways, the Globetrotters served as basketball's first ambassadors, spreading the game's appeal far and wide.

Beyond their on-court antics and basketball prowess, the Globetrotters also played a significant role in social change. During a time when America was grappling with segregation and racial inequality, the Globetrotters were breaking down racial barriers, one game at a time. They played in front of racially integrated audiences, something that was still rare in many parts of the United States and the world during the early years of the team's existence. Their success and popularity challenged prevailing racial prejudices and demonstrated the folly of segregation, contributing to the gradual change in societal attitudes.

The Globetrotters' influence extended to the world of professional basketball as well. Many of their players, such as Wilt Chamberlain, one of the greatest basketball players of all time, went on to have successful careers in the NBA. The skills and showmanship that the Globetrotters brought to the court influenced how the game was played and presented, adding an element of entertainment that has become a staple of modern basketball.

The Harlem Globetrotters have not only been pioneers in blending sports with entertainment but also instrumental in fostering important social changes and promoting goodwill across the globe. Their tours, often to places where professional basketball was unheard of, served as a bridge between diverse cultures, showcasing the uniting power of sports.

One of the most poignant aspects of the Globetrotters' legacy is their role in promoting racial integration in sports. In the mid-20th century, when segregation was still prevalent in the United States, the Globetrotters were drawing mixed-race crowds to their games, challenging societal norms and prejudices. Their games became events where the color of one's skin didn't matter, only the shared joy of the game. This not only showcased the absurdity of segregation but also highlighted the team's role in the larger civil rights movement.

The Globetrotters' influence extended into breaking down international barriers as well. During the Cold War, a time of heightened tensions between the United States and the Soviet Union, the Globetrotters played in Moscow. Their visit, marked by goodwill and the common language of basketball, demonstrated the potential for sports to transcend political and ideological divides. The team received a warm reception, and for a brief moment, basketball overcame the Cold War's chill, fostering a sense of shared humanity.

The players who made up the Harlem Globetrotters over the years each brought their unique flair and talent to the team, becoming legends in their own right. From Goose Tatum, often regarded as the original "Clown Prince" of the Globetrotters, to Fred "Curly" Neal, whose bald head and dribbling wizardry made him one of the most recognizable Globetrotters, the team was always a blend of diverse talents and personalities. Each player not only contributed to the team's success on the court but also to its enduring legacy off it.

The Globetrotters' influence on basketball's development and presentation is undeniable. Their flair for theatrics and emphasis on entertainment have seeped into professional basketball, making the sport not just a competitive endeavor but also a spectacle. The NBA, with its high-flying dunks, no-look passes, and charismatic stars, owes a part of its appeal to the trail blazed by the Globetrotters.

The Harlem Globetrotters' journey through the decades is a vivid tapestry of memorable moments, groundbreaking achievements, and profound social impact, continuing to resonate with fans and communities worldwide. Their legacy is not just built on the victories and laughter they've brought to countless spectators but also on their unwavering commitment to making a difference, both on and off the court.

In recent years, the Globetrotters have remained at the forefront of using their platform to advocate for social issues, including racial equality, children's welfare, and education. Their initiatives extend beyond the game, involving community outreach programs, charity events, and educational workshops, demonstrating the team's holistic approach to their role as global ambassadors of basketball and goodwill.

The Globetrotters' style of play, a mesmerizing blend of athleticism and comedy, continues to evolve, incorporating modern basketball techniques while maintaining the essence of the entertainment and joy that have been their trademarks. This evolution ensures that their performances remain relevant and engaging for new generations of fans, keeping the spirit of the original Globetrotters alive.

The team's interaction with the audience remains a hallmark of their shows, breaking the fourth wall that typically exists in professional sports. This direct engagement creates a unique experience for spectators, making each Globetrotter game a personal and memorable event. It's this connection with the audience that has helped cement the Globetrotters' place in the hearts of fans around the world.

Moreover, the Harlem Globetrotters' influence on the world of sports entertainment has paved the way for similar concepts in other sports, showing that the combination of elite skill and entertainment has a universal appeal. Their impact can be seen in the rise of entertaining sports leagues and events that prioritize fan engagement and entertainment alongside athletic competition.

The Harlem Globetrotters' influence extends beyond the traditional realms of professional basketball, inspiring various forms of basketball entertainment that combine athleticism with showmanship. One notable example of this legacy is the And1 Mixtape Tour, a streetball tour that gained popularity in the late 1990s and early 2000s. The And1 Mixtape Tour showcased the skills and flair of streetball players, emphasizing creativity, ball-handling, and crowd-pleasing moves, much in the spirit of what the Globetrotters have been doing for decades.

The Globetrotters, with their emphasis on entertainment and engaging the audience through basketball, laid the groundwork for the And1 Mixtape Tour's success. The tour's players, much like the Globetrotters, were known for their unique nicknames, incredible dribbling skills, and the ability to perform seemingly impossible shots and dunks. This style of play, where the entertainment value is as important as the athleticism, can be traced back to the Globetrotters' innovative approach to the game.

Furthermore, the Globetrotters' tradition of involving the audience in their performances, making each game an interactive experience, can be seen in the way And1 Mixtape Tour events were structured. Fans were not just spectators but became part of the show, with players frequently engaging with them directly, similar to the Globetrotters' long-standing practice of bringing fans onto the court for comedic bits or to assist in trick shots.

It's evident that the Harlem Globetrotters' impact on basketball and sports entertainment is profound and far-reaching. From inspiring other basketball entertainment tours to breaking down racial and cultural barriers, the Globetrotters have solidified their place in history not just as a basketball team but as cultural icons. Their legacy continues to inspire, entertain, and bring joy to audiences around the world, proving that the Harlem Globetrotters are truly in a league of their own.

Chapter 14:
The First Great Rivalry: Bill Russell vs. Wilt Chamberlain

∞

Few basketball rivalries are as legendary and transformative as the one between Bill Russell of the Boston Celtics and Wilt Chamberlain, who played for several teams including the Philadelphia/San Francisco Warriors and the Los Angeles Lakers. This epic rivalry between two of the game's greatest centers not only captivated fans but also fundamentally changed how basketball was played and perceived.

Bill Russell was known for his incredible defensive skills, unmatched basketball IQ, and leadership on the court. His ability to read the game and make crucial plays made him the cornerstone of the Boston Celtics' dynasty in the 1950s and 1960s. Russell's approach to the game was all about teamwork, selflessness, and doing whatever it took to win. He wasn't just playing to score points; he was playing to lift his entire team and secure victory.

On the other side was Wilt Chamberlain, a player of immense talent and physical prowess. Chamberlain was an offensive powerhouse, known for his scoring ability, rebounding, and dominance in the paint. He was the kind of player who could change the course of a game single-handedly, setting records that still stand today, including scoring 100 points in a single game.

The rivalry between Russell and Chamberlain was about more than just two players going head-to-head; it was a clash of philosophies, styles, and visions for how basketball could be played. Russell's Celtics were all about precision, teamwork, and a defense-first approach, while Chamberlain's teams often relied on his individual brilliance to overpower opponents.

Their matchups were eagerly anticipated events, drawing fans from all over to witness these two giants of the game battle it out on the court. Each game was a chess match, with Russell trying to outsmart and outmaneuver Chamberlain, and Chamberlain using his strength and skill to dominate the scoreboard. The intensity and competitiveness of their encounters brought out the best in both players, pushing them to new heights and etching their rivalry into the history books.

Beyond the games, the rivalry between Russell and Chamberlain was marked by mutual respect and camaraderie. Off the court, they were friends, sharing laughs and conversations, a testament to the sportsmanship and character of both men. This friendship added another layer to their rivalry, showcasing that even the fiercest competitors can have admiration and respect for each other.

The rivalry between Bill Russell and Wilt Chamberlain wasn't just confined to the regular NBA season; it reached its pinnacle during the playoffs and, most notably, the NBA Finals. These high-stakes encounters provided the perfect backdrop for their legendary duels, as both players were not only battling for personal pride but also for the ultimate team accolade - the NBA Championship.

Russell's Celtics and Chamberlain's teams faced off numerous times in the playoffs, creating a narrative filled with tension, drama, and unforgettable basketball moments. One of the most notable series took place in the 1960s, a decade dominated by the Celtics but consistently challenged by Chamberlain's formidable presence. Each playoff game between Russell and Chamberlain was a masterclass in basketball, showcasing Russell's strategic defense against Chamberlain's offensive onslaught.

In these epic battles, Russell often focused on leveraging his team's strengths, using his defensive acumen to orchestrate the Celtics' resistance against Chamberlain. His philosophy was rooted in the belief that basketball is a team sport, and success could only be achieved through unity and collective effort. This approach was evident in how the Celtics played, with every member contributing to both ends of the court, embodying the essence of teamwork and collaboration.

On the other hand, Chamberlain, with his incredible scoring ability, often carried the weight of his team's offensive expectations. His battles with Russell were not just physical but also mental, as each sought to outwit and outplay the other. Chamberlain's performances in these playoff series were a testament to his skill and determination, often pushing Russell and the Celtics to their limits.

The rivalry between Russell and Chamberlain also highlighted the evolution of the center position in basketball. They transformed what it meant to be a big man in the NBA, combining size with skill, intelligence, and an unparalleled understanding of the game. Their matchups were a showcase of how the center position could influence both the offensive and defensive aspects of the game, setting new standards for future generations of players.

The respect between Russell and Chamberlain grew with each encounter. Despite their fierce battles, they shared a mutual admiration that transcended the competition. This respect was rooted in the recognition of each other's talents and the shared experiences of being African American athletes during a time of significant social change in the United States. Their friendship off the court was a powerful reminder of the respect and camaraderie that can exist between competitors.

The Russell-Chamberlain rivalry was not only about their personal matchups but also how they elevated their teams and the sport of basketball. Each game they played was a lesson in excellence, determination, and the pursuit of greatness. Their encounters were eagerly awaited by fans, creating a buzz and excitement that packed arenas and captivated television audiences across the nation.

Bill Russell's leadership and defensive prowess were instrumental in the Boston Celtics' remarkable run of 11 championships in 13 seasons, a feat unmatched in the history of professional sports. Russell's approach to the game, emphasizing defense, teamwork, and selflessness, became the blueprint for success in the NBA. His ability to motivate his teammates, to lead by example, and to make game-changing plays on the defensive end of the floor were hallmarks of the Celtics' dynasty.

Wilt Chamberlain, with his record-setting performances, brought a new level of excitement and individual achievement to the game. Chamberlain's scoring feats, including his legendary 100-point game, were not just personal triumphs but milestones that pushed the boundaries of what was considered possible in basketball. His dominance on the court forced teams to innovate and adapt, changing the way basketball was played and defended.

The rivalry between Russell and Chamberlain also had a significant cultural impact, transcending the boundaries of the basketball court. During a time of significant social and racial upheaval in the United States, they were towering African American figures in a predominantly white league, breaking down barriers and setting an example for future generations. Their success and conduct on and off the court played a part in the broader struggle for civil rights and equality, offering hope and inspiration to countless individuals.

The legacy of the Russell-Chamberlain rivalry lives on in the NBA today. Current players and fans look back at their epic battles as defining moments in the sport's history, drawing inspiration from their dedication, skill, and sportsmanship. The lessons learned from their rivalry—about competition, respect, and the pursuit of excellence—are as relevant today as they were during the height of their careers.

Beyond the intense matchups and the championship battles, the Russell-Chamberlain rivalry was enriched by the personal growth and mutual respect that developed between the two legends over the years. As fierce as their competition was on the court, off the court, they shared moments that highlighted their humanity and the depth of their characters.

One such moment came after Bill Russell retired. Wilt Chamberlain, who had often been criticized for not winning as many championships as Russell, found in his rival a defender. Russell publicly stated that judging Chamberlain's career solely on the number of championships won was unfair, emphasizing Wilt's incredible contributions to the game and his unparalleled skill set. This act of camaraderie from Russell, even after their competitive years had ended, demonstrated the profound respect they had for each other's talents and achievements.

Their relationship also showcased the complexities of being sports icons in a rapidly changing America. Both Russell and Chamberlain were prominent African American figures during the civil rights era, using their platforms to advocate for social justice and equality. They navigated the challenges of racism and discrimination, both in and out of the sports arena, with dignity and strength. Their experiences and actions off the court contributed significantly to the progress of African American athletes in professional sports and beyond.

The Russell-Chamberlain rivalry also left a lasting impact on the NBA, influencing how centers were perceived and utilized in the game. They transformed the role of the center from a primarily defensive position to one that could also be a major offensive threat. Their battles in the paint changed team strategies, leading to innovations in coaching and playing styles that took into account the need to defend against and utilize dominant centers effectively.

The legacy of their rivalry is a testament to the power of sports to inspire and unite. The excitement and anticipation surrounding their matchups brought fans together, creating shared memories that have lasted a lifetime. The respect and friendship that Russell and Chamberlain shared, despite their on-court battles, serve as a powerful reminder of the values of sportsmanship, respect, and the unifying power of basketball.

Chapter 15:
Shaquille O'Neal: The Most
Dominant Center Ever

∞

In the vast galaxy of basketball stars, Shaquille O'Neal, or "Shaq" as he is affectionately known, shines brightly as one of the most dominant centers to ever play the game. With his towering presence, incredible strength, and charismatic personality, Shaq left an indelible mark on the NBA and captured the hearts of fans around the world.

Shaq's journey to basketball greatness began in Newark, New Jersey, where he was born. From a young age, it was clear that Shaq was destined for greatness. As he grew, so did his love for basketball, and by the time he was in high school, Shaq was already a force to be reckoned with on the court. His combination of size, agility, and skill made him a standout player, and it wasn't long before colleges across the nation took notice.

Shaq decided to take his talents to Louisiana State University (LSU), where he quickly became a sensation. At LSU, Shaq dominated the college basketball scene with his powerful dunks, shot-blocking prowess, and rebounding ability. He was not just a big player; he was an agile athlete who could run the floor, handle the ball, and outmaneuver opponents with surprising grace for his size.

After an illustrious college career, Shaq entered the NBA Draft and was selected as the first overall pick by the Orlando Magic in 1992. From the moment he stepped onto the NBA court, Shaq's impact was immediate and profound. He was named the Rookie of the Year and quickly became one of the most feared players in the league.

Shaq's dominance on the court was unmatched. He had a unique blend of power and finesse that allowed him to overpower defenders and score with ease. His signature "Shaq Attack" - a powerful dunk that often left opponents and backboards in shambles - became a symbol of his dominance. But Shaq wasn't just about strength; he had a soft touch around the rim and a variety of post moves that made him nearly impossible to defend.

Throughout his career, Shaq played for several teams, including the Los Angeles Lakers, Miami Heat, Phoenix Suns, Cleveland Cavaliers, and Boston Celtics. However, it was with the Lakers that Shaq achieved his greatest success. Alongside Kobe Bryant, Shaq led the Lakers to three consecutive NBA Championships from 2000 to 2002, earning Finals MVP honors each time. His partnership with Kobe became one of the most iconic duos in NBA history, combining Shaq's inside dominance with Kobe's skill and competitiveness.

Off the court, Shaq was just as larger-than-life. His playful personality, sense of humor, and love for entertainment endeared him to fans and made him a media favorite. Shaq dabbled in acting, music, and even law enforcement, showcasing his diverse interests and talents beyond basketball.

Shaq's dominance on the basketball court was not just about his physical attributes; it was also about his basketball IQ and understanding of the game. He knew how to use his size and strength to his advantage, positioning himself in ways that made him nearly unstoppable. Defenders often had no choice but to foul him, leading to what became known as the "Hack-a-Shaq" strategy, where teams would intentionally foul Shaq, hoping he would miss his free throws. Despite this, Shaq's scoring ability, combined with his defensive presence, made him a key player on any team he was part of.

During his time with the Lakers, Shaq's partnership with coach Phil Jackson was instrumental in the team's success. Jackson's "triangle offense" allowed Shaq to maximize his effectiveness on the court, creating opportunities for him and his teammates. Shaq's ability to draw double teams opened up the floor for his teammates, making the Lakers' offense one of the most potent in the league.

Shaq's move to the Miami Heat in 2004 marked a new chapter in his career. Teaming up with Dwyane Wade, Shaq helped lead the Heat to their first-ever NBA Championship in 2006. This victory was a testament to Shaq's leadership and his ability to elevate the play of those around him. Even as he adapted to a new team and a new role, Shaq's impact was undeniable, proving that he was more than just a dominant center; he was a winner.

Shaq's influence extended beyond his own teams. He changed the way the center position was played, inspiring a generation of players to develop a more versatile skill set. His combination of size, athleticism, and skill challenged the traditional view of big men as primarily defensive players, paving the way for the modern NBA, where centers are expected to contribute in multiple facets of the game.

Shaq's charisma made him a beloved figure in popular culture. His appearances in movies, television shows, and commercials, along with his rap albums, showcased his personality and his ability to connect with people in various entertainment mediums. Shaq's philanthropic efforts, particularly his work with children's charities, further endeared him to fans, highlighting his commitment to giving back to the community.

Shaq's journey in the NBA was punctuated by memorable moments that highlighted his unique blend of skill, strength, and personality. One such moment came during the 2000 NBA Finals against the Indiana Pacers, where Shaq's performance was nothing short of historic. Dominating both ends of the court, he averaged 38 points and 16.7 rebounds per game throughout the series, showcasing his unmatched ability to influence the game's outcome. This series solidified Shaq's reputation as a clutch performer and a player who rose to the occasion when the stakes were highest.

Beyond his individual achievements, Shaq's ability to make his teammates better was one of his most significant contributions to the game. Whether it was setting bone-crushing screens, passing out of double teams to find the open man, or simply drawing so much attention that his teammates had more space to operate, Shaq's presence on the court elevated the play of those around him. This team-first mentality, despite his superstar status, endeared him to his teammates and coaches alike.

Shaq's influence on the game extended to the defensive end as well. His ability to protect the rim and alter shots made opposing players think twice before driving to the basket. Shaq's defensive prowess was not just about blocking shots; it was about imposing his will and making opponents adjust their game plans to account for his presence in the paint.

Shaq's retirement from professional basketball in 2011 marked the end of an era, but his impact on the game remains. Today, Shaq is a successful sports analyst, where his insights into the game, combined with his charismatic delivery, make him a beloved figure in the basketball community. His transition from an NBA superstar to a media personality has been seamless, showcasing his versatility and ability to connect with people in various capacities.

Shaq's dominance in the NBA reshaped the center position, blending size and strength with agility and skill in a way that had never been seen before. His ability to dominate games established a new standard for what it meant to be a "big man" in the league, inspiring a generation of players to emulate his style and approach to the game. Shaq's influence helped to popularize basketball globally, making it accessible and enjoyable to fans of all ages and backgrounds.

Shaq's journey from a dynamic, dominant center to a beloved cultural icon is a testament to his hard work, determination, and the joy he brought to everything he did. His legacy is not just about the championships, records, or accolades, but about the way he inspired people to believe in themselves, to pursue their passions, and to enjoy life to the fullest.

In reflecting on his career, we celebrate a player who was not only the most dominant center ever to grace the NBA but also a person who brought laughter, joy, and inspiration to millions around the world. Shaq's story reminds us that greatness comes in many forms, and his contributions to basketball and society will be remembered for generations to come.

Made in the USA
Middletown, DE
14 December 2024

67085116R00066